# HUTTERITE DIARIES

## PLAINSPOKEN

*Real-life stories of Amish and Mennonites*

"Linda Maendel's clear vision and her loving heart wrapped me in a fine quilt of story as I read. Of all of the books on Hutterites that I have seen, this is the one that I cherish."
— Joe McLellan, author of the Nanabosho series

"This book will awaken your longing for a better world. As I read it, I smiled, laughed out loud, and cried along with the author and her community. Linda Maendel takes you deep into Hutterian community life one gentle picture at a time."
— Shirley Hershey Showalter, author of *Blush*

"*Hutterite Diaries* is an insightful look into Hutterite colony life from an insider who not only describes what life is like there but why things are done in particular ways. Maendel's explanations will not only resonate with all Hutterites but also provide an important introduction to Hutterite life for non-Hutterites."
— Rod Janzen, author of *The Hutterites in North America*

"*Hutterite Diaries* is a welcome and long overdue contribution that fills a void in the daily events of a Hutterite. This book reveals a way of life that seems extraordinary to the outside world."
— Paul M. Wipf, farm steward, Viking Hutterite Colony

"I so much enjoyed the chance to step into the Hutterite community and feel a part of it. Linda Maendel's delightful use of the power of story makes the *Hutterite Diaries* the type of book that is universal and enduring."
— Sigmund Brouwer, author of *Thief of Glory*

"What an amazing book! Informative, interesting, entertaining, and very well written. Through skillfully told stories, Linda Maendel, an insider, guides the reader on a journey exploring the world of a Hutterite community. Her book provides an important addition to the literature now available about Hutterite life."
— John J. Friesen, professor emeritus, Canadian Mennonite University

# HUTTERITE DIARIES

*Wisdom from My Prairie Community*

## LINDA MAENDEL

**Herald Press**

Harrisonburg, Virginia
Kitchener, Ontario

**Library of Congress Cataloging-in-Publication Data**
Maendel, Linda, 1962-
  Hutterite diaries : wisdom from my prairie community / Linda Maendel.
    pages cm. -- (Plainspoken: real-life stories of Amish and other plain Christians)
    ISBN 978-0-8361-9946-8 (pbk. : alk. paper)  1.  Hutterian Brethren--United
States. 2.  Hutterian Brethren--United States--Social life and customs.  I. Title.
  BX8129.H8M34 2015
  289.7'3--dc23

                                  2015003491

Some chapters in this book previously appeared in other publications: "Beehive Busyness" appeared in *Portage Daily Graphic* and *Manitoba Cooperator*; "Weathered Wood Lessons" in the *Portage Daily Graphic* and *Winnipeg Free Press*; "Hearts and Hand for Common Causes" in the *Manitoba Cooperator*; sections of "Christmas on the Colony" in *Winnipeg Free Press* and *Lamplight Tales*, a Poetry Institute of Canada short story anthology; "Lenten Reflection" in *Portage Daily Graphic*; and "Bracing for the Breach" in *Winnipeg Free Press* and *Our Canada*.

HUTTERITE DIARIES
© 2015 by Herald Press, Kitchener, Ontario N2G 3R1
  Released simultaneously in USA by Herald Press,
  Harrisonburg, Virginia 22802. All rights reserved.
Library of Congress Control Number: 2015003491
International Standard Book Number: 978-0-8361-9946-8
Printed in United States of America
Cover and interior design by Reuben Graham
Cover photo by Linda Maendel

Photo credits: Sonia Maendel, pp. 27, 29, 34, 70, 108, 109; Linda Maendel, pp. 99, 102, 105, 147, 149; Kenny Wollman, p. 58; Susan Sevig, p. 133; Judith Maendel, pp. 50, 52; Erol Kagan, p. 139

Scriptures taken from the *Holy Bible, New International Version*®. © 1973, 1978, 1984, 2011 by Biblica, Inc.™ Used by permission of Zondervan. All rights reserved worldwide. www.zondervan.com The "NIV" and "New International Version" are trademarks registered in the United States Patent and Trademark Office by Biblica, Inc.™

To order or request information, please call 1-800-245-7894. Or visit www.heraldpress.com.

19 18 17 16 15          10 9 8 7 6 5 4 3 2 1

*To my fellow Hutterites,*
*in hopes that it will inspire many*
*to pen their stories*
*and have the courage to publish them.*

*Nowhere is a sincere believer happier than in the presence of his brothers and fellow believers. They show each other love, reverence, and faithfulness and do good to each other. It is the divine nature of love that makes us feel we are in our neighbor's debt and urges us to serve him joyfully where we can. Brothers and sisters refresh each other by sharing the gifts God put into their hearts for the good of the Body of Christ, which is the gathering of all the believers who have made a common bond in God's love.*

—Claus Felbinger, sixteenth-century Hutterite martyr,
from *Brotherly Community, Highest Command of Love*

# Contents

*Introduction to Plainspoken* . . . . . . . . . . . . . . . . . . . . . . . . . . 9
*A Day in the Life of the Author.* . . . . . . . . . . . . . . . . . . . . . . 11

**PART I: FELLOWSHIP**

1. Beehive Busyness . . . . . . . . . . . . . . . . . . . . . . . . . . . . . . . 25
2. Beauty in the Ashes . . . . . . . . . . . . . . . . . . . . . . . . . . . . . 33
3. Life Lessons from Grandpa . . . . . . . . . . . . . . . . . . . . . 39
4. A Circle Not Unbroken . . . . . . . . . . . . . . . . . . . . . . . . 45
5. Trotting on Trust. . . . . . . . . . . . . . . . . . . . . . . . . . . . . . 49
6. To Write a Hutterite Story . . . . . . . . . . . . . . . . . . . . . 55
7. Two Empty Chairs . . . . . . . . . . . . . . . . . . . . . . . . . . . . 61

**PART II: CELEBRATIONS**

8. Marriages Strengthened by Community . . . . . . . . . . . . 67
9. Christmas on the Colony. . . . . . . . . . . . . . . . . . . . . . . . 73
10. Sisterly Love—Laced with Revenge . . . . . . . . . . . . . . . 79
11. Lenten Reflection . . . . . . . . . . . . . . . . . . . . . . . . . . . . . 83
12. A Peaches and Cream Mother's Day . . . . . . . . . . . . . . . 89

## PART III: VALUES

13. Weathered Wood Lessons . . . . . . . . . . . . . . . . . . . . . . . . 95
14. Hearts and Hands for Common Causes . . . . . . . . . . . . 101
15. Bracing for the Breach . . . . . . . . . . . . . . . . . . . . . . . . . . 107
16. Hospitality in a Time of War . . . . . . . . . . . . . . . . . . . . . 113
17. God Keep Our Land Glorious and Free . . . . . . . . . . . . . 121
18. Steel Bar Blues . . . and Blessings . . . . . . . . . . . . . . . . . . 125

## PART IV: HERITAGE

19. The Amana-Hutterite Connection . . . . . . . . . . . . . . . . . 131
20. A Hutterite Story of Slavery . . . . . . . . . . . . . . . . . . . . . . 137
21. Following the Footsteps of Our Forebears . . . . . . . . . . 145
22. Love without End . . . . . . . . . . . . . . . . . . . . . . . . . . . . . . 151

FAQs about the Hutterites: The Author Answers . . . . . . . . . . 155
Author's Note . . . . . . . . . . . . . . . . . . . . . . . . . . . . . . . . . . . . 163
The Author . . . . . . . . . . . . . . . . . . . . . . . . . . . . . . . . . . . . . . 165

# INTRODUCTION TO

P L A I N S P O K E N

*Real-life stories of Amish and Mennonites*

**N**OVELS, TOURIST SITES, AND TELEVISION SHOWS offer second- or third-hand accounts of Amish, Mennonite, and Hutterite life. Some of these messages are sensitive and accurate. Some are not. Many are flat-out wrong.

Now readers can listen directly to the voices of these Anabaptists themselves through Plainspoken. In the books in this series, readers get to hear Amish, Mennonite, and Hutterite writers talk about the texture of their daily lives: how they spend their time, what they value, what makes them laugh, and how they summon strength from their Christian faith and community.

Plain Anabaptists are publishing their writing more than ever before. But this literature is read mostly by other Amish, Mennonites, and Hutterites, and rarely by the larger public.

Through Plainspoken, readers outside their communities can learn what authentic plain Anabaptist life looks and feels like—from the inside out. The Amish and Mennonites and Hutterites have stories to tell. Through Plainspoken, readers get the chance to hear them.

# A Day in the Life of the Author

*What a teacher writes on the blackboard*
*of life can never be erased.*

—Author unknown

**7:15 a.m.** I walk leisurely to the communal kitchen for breakfast, soaking up the morning air and the surrounding splendor. Autumn has painted trees and shrubs in shades of orange, yellow, and red, and some leaves have escaped onto the neatly trimmed, still-green lawns. Dew-kissed grass blades sparkle as if somebody shattered crystals.

"Good morning!" I greet a groggy teenager as he drags his half-awake self in the same direction.

"What's so good about it?" he grunts. The crisp fall air and my incredulous look shake the last traces of sleep from him and he adds, "Save the lecture! I know: beautiful day, I'm alive and healthy, with a great place to live." Straightening his shoulders some and walking more briskly, he chirps, "Good morning!"

"Much better!" I smile. He holds the kitchen door for me.

From the *smorg* (a buffet-style table) in the dining room, I get a perfectly baked whole wheat pancake and coffee and take my place. Traditionally, Hutterite men sit on one side of the room and women on the other. Every Christmas, though, we all enjoy sitting with our families. A few days after the holiday, we are happy to return to the usual seating order.

*7:30 a.m.* After the minister asks the blessing, I pour homemade maple syrup on my pancake and savor my breakfast. Soon my mind wanders to my favorite pastime: writing. Recently Herald Press asked me whether I'd be interested in writing a book for their Plainspoken series. I begin to reflect about how I would describe my writing and whether such a description would be a good contribution to the series. *What am I writing about?* I muse, as I take a sip of coffee. I'm journaling about living on a Hutterite colony; each story or article is a glimpse of my communal life. Creating word pictures is like collecting treasures; it makes me take a closer look at aspects of my life. Via my blog and newspaper articles, I get to share my musings with people around the world.

I savor the last mouthful of my perfectly baked pancake. Perhaps the time is right to compile my writings into a book. After all, haven't we as Hutterites grappled long enough with the idea of telling our own stories? When others write about us, things tend to get twisted, either intentionally or because the author couldn't grasp certain aspects of our communal life. As a result, outside writers put their own spin on it. Sadly, though, once published, their writing is often taken as the truth. Now a door is opening to tell our own story. I feel inclined to enter it; as my dad used to say, *"Wer nix praviet, der gwinnt ach nix"* (Nothing ventured, nothing gained).

"*Mir wean donkn.*" Breaking through my reverie, the minister signals the prayer of thanks offered after every meal. "*Gott Lob und Dank, für Speis und Trank . . .*" (Praise and thanks to God for food and drink).

Not on dishwashing duty this week, I leave my dishes in the kitchen and head home. I need to pick up some books for school.

**8:00 a.m.** My workday starts. For many years our colony school has been blessed with our own people as trained teachers. Ours is considered a public school; thus all teachers, including me, are hired by the Portage la Prairie School Division. Every colony has its own Hutterite German teachers and most have non-Hutterite teachers. Many, however, have their own Hutterite people, with degrees in education, who teach on the colony.

I'm an educational assistant, hired half time and working full time with grades K–8 students. Over the years, I obtained my grade twelve general education diploma and have taken some university courses. Twice I've studied in Germany; the first time, I took a German language course; more recently, I studied teaching methods.

I arrive at school along with the first students. Some come on foot, others on scooters or bicycles. Once inside, they're as chirpy as the sparrows perched on the trees near the school. "Linda, I was at the dentist yesterday and I didn't cry," little Sophia informs me with a gap-toothed grin.

"Good for you!" I tease. "I see he took your front teeth."

"No, he didn't," she giggles; "They fell out on their own. My mom says everybody loses all their baby teeth. Then new ones grow."

We start our day with morning devotions, a song, a Bible story, and a prayer. Our song, "*Erwacht vom süßen Schlummer*" calls us to praise God after a peaceful and restful night. "Just like one of the ten lepers in today's Bible story," I explain to my young students, "we too need to always have a grateful heart."

"Yesterday, my mom wasn't feeling well, and I helped her with the dishes," Doreen remembers. "She said, 'Thank you very much. You are a good little helper.'"

**8:20 a.m.** We spread out to various classrooms to tackle German, mathematics, language arts, and other subjects outlined in the Manitoba curriculum. Every day until noon, I teach kindergarten. This year I have a class of five: three girls and two boys.

My first class is German. All Hutterite children start school knowing mostly Hutterisch, a Carinthian German dialect originating from the province of Carinthia in Austria. While children may have been exposed to German and English with songs and stories, it's only at age five years that they learn both these languages in earnest. This causes some confusion for them at school, especially in the first few years, but eventually they sort it all out and begin to understand their two additional languages.

Living in an English-speaking country, we're simply more exposed to that language on a daily basis, so it comes easier. German always proves to be more challenging, though, since there's seldom an opportunity to speak it outside the school setting, even though it is part of our heritage and most of our sermons and all the singing in church are done in German. I relish every chance I get to speak German; this includes hosting friends from German-speaking countries, Skyping with them, and sometimes visiting them.

**9:00 a.m.** We switch to math. Today we're working with ten-frames: rectangles that have two rows of five squares each, used to teach early number sense. I call a number between one and ten, and the students place bingo chips on their blank ten-frame sheet. It's always exciting to watch these little ones as their minds figure out how to change quickly from one number to the next. The first number is eight. Some meticulously count out each number, but one boy already knows exactly how many chips one ten-frame holds, which naturally helps him get done faster. My next number is three, and I'm thrilled that with one swipe of the hand the same boy moves some chips off the ten-frame, leaving exactly three.

"Wow! How did you do this so quickly?" I ask.

"I just know it. My brain told me," he answers, unable to explain the process.

**10:00 a.m.** As the bird clock on my classroom wall chirps ten, my students scamper for recess. "Listen, everybody!" Daniel announces in his booming voice. "Let's play hide-and-seek again."

After a twenty-minute break, my five eager students enjoy learning the alphabet through songs, gestures, drawings, and stories. At the end of each morning I give them playtime, during which they get to choose from a variety of activities, such as jigsaw puzzles or Legos. Hearing the conversations during that time is like getting ice cream on a piece of Saskatoon pie. I've often said they should be recorded.

Take the day the chattiest girl in the bunch admonished one of the boys. "You better not talk so much or your mouth will break," she told him. "That's what my mom always says to me."

Unwilling to accept admonition from Miss Chatterbox, he retorted, "Then why isn't your mouth broken yet?"

**11:30 a.m.** A lively tune on the public address system calls students to the children's dining room, at the communal kitchen. After their meal the older children babysit while the adults come and have their lunch at twelve. Today we're having my favorite traditional Hutterite meal: borscht and *Knedl* with chicken and steamed vegetables. I always wonder if Hutterites picked up the recipe for borscht during their time in Russia, before coming to America in the late 1800s. Or did they enjoy this delicious soup before then? *Knedl* are made from a mixture of water, flour, leftover cooked potatoes, and a pinch of salt, cut into big chunks and boiled. After they're cooled, they are ground into crumbles and fried on a skillet. Most often people add *Knedl* to their borscht, but some eat them separately as well. One simply cannot buy a meal like this anywhere!

While I eat, I'm reminded of a cute conversation I was privy to earlier. All five of my kindergartners, three girls and two boys, were playing house when an argument ensued. They couldn't decide who would be married to whom—two of the girls had their heart set on the same boy. Just as I was going to intervene and in some way help settle this dispute, one girl, with hands on her hips, adamantly stated, "If you want to be a woman in this house, you can be Grandma." Her tone of voice and no-nonsense manner had me turning my back so that they wouldn't see me laughing. Amazingly, this announcement instantly restored peace.

And why not? Who wouldn't want to be Grandma, who knits the best slippers in the world and has a stash of candies tucked away especially for the *Eniklen,* her dear grandchildren?

***12:30 p.m.*** I'm back in school and settling in with a group of students in grades four to seven, who at times are not terribly excited about German lessons. This is a stark contrast from the eager bunch I spend my mornings with. However, on this day, this group of older children are on the edge of their seats as I read the last chapter of *Steinadler,* the German version of *Stone Fox* by John Reynolds. While they are delighted that Stone Fox, the old Indian, helps Willy win the race, they are disappointed that the story ends so abruptly. "*Aw,* I wanted to see Willy celebrate the win with his sick grandpa," one seventh-grader laments, "especially since the prize money will save their farm."

"Ending the story abruptly is a tactic some authors use to keep your mind going even after the last sentence has been read," I explain. "Listening to your ideas, I'm convinced that this method works. Perhaps we could do a written response on how you would like this story to end."

My suggestion is greeted with a collective groan, as if a severe case of indigestion has just set in on the entire group.

***1:15 p.m.*** I have a forty-five minute reading class with students in grades one to three. On a rotating basis, students practice various literary activities: reading independently, reading with a partner, reading to the teacher, and spending time at the listening center. The last ten minutes I read to them. At the moment they are completely captivated with Suzanne Woods Fisher's *A Surprise for Lily.* In many ways, they can relate to the values of the little Amish girl in the story: faith, strong family ties, a fun-filled farm life, and modest dress.

When people see photographs of Hutterites, they sometimes think we're Amish. We're not, but we are part of the same Christian faith family: the Anabaptists, who emerged in the 1500s in Europe. Like the Amish, we emphasize simplicity, nonconformity to the world, adult baptism, separation of church and state, and nonresistance. More than other Anabaptist groups, however, we emphasize sharing of material goods, following the example of the believers in the early church, who "had everything in common" (Acts 2:44) and "shared everything they had" (Acts 4:32).

Since our Anabaptist beginnings, we Hutterites, like the Amish, have practiced a modest, simple, and uniform dress code. The early traditional style originates from the German and Austrian national dress: black *Lederhosen* and suspenders for men and boys, and the *Dirndl*, a sleeveless dress with a blouse and an apron, for women and girls. Over the years, Hutterites have modified these to make them more serviceable and comfortable. This outward symbol of unity and modesty is an integral part of our faith life, identifying and reminding us of who we are as a people.

There are three distinct groups of Hutterites: *Dariusleut*, *Lehrerleut*, and *Schmiedeleut*, each adhering to its own variations of this dress code. Similarities among the groups include blouses and ankle-length dresses along with a *Tiechl* (a head covering) for women, and dark pants and suspenders for men. Both men and women usually wear dark jackets or coats in cold weather. Children wear lighter colors than adults, and in all three groups, little girls wear a head covering known as a *Mitz*, or bonnet.

I belong to the *Schmiedeleut*, the most progressive of the three groups. The name was derived from the German word for blacksmith, *Schmied*. In the early 1800s, for forty years, Hutterites abandoned the practice of living communally. Michael Hofer, a blacksmith also known as *Schmied Michel*, along with Darius Walter and Jacob Hofer, renewed the community of goods once more.

*Schmiedeleut* men wear many types of casual jackets, mostly dark-colored. Their suit jackets are similar to those that non-Hutterites would wear, and in most cases they are homemade. Women wear either a two-piece or one-piece dress, in a wide variety of colors and prints, according to preference. The *Tiechl* is mostly plain black. In some colonies women wear a sheer black apron to church services, though most have eliminated it.

For Hutterites, the goal is modest, simple clothing in uniform style, according to the church ordinances of each *Leut* (conference). Dressing differently from mainstream society is as much a part of Hutterianism as living communally, and it fosters a sense of belonging to a much larger whole. In the spirit of the New Testament teaching that exhorts believers to strive for the inner beauty that produces a wealth of good works (1 Peter 3:1-6), this is a testimony that not only benefits others but pleases and honors God.

*2:15 p.m.* Last period on this day I have no classes, so I use it for prep time and to mark the work of students. By four thirty I call it a day and head home to relax with a cup of coffee and piece of freshly baked *Zucker Honkelich*, a scrumptious, creamy sugar pie.

And all is well with the world— especially when my two pre-school nephews, Jakobi and Terrance, bounce into our house, wanting to hear a story or play with their toys. I spend a few minutes with them and then cozy up to my computer. I am soon lost in my own wonderful writing world and working on a fascinating story, linked to our Hutterite history, for my blog. It's about Hutterite descendants, freed slaves from the 1605 Turkish War, whom nobody ever knew about until recently.

Before I know it, it's time to get ready for *Gebet*, the evening church service.

**6:00 p.m.** Our minister leads us in a German evening song: "*Ich danke dir, liebreicher Gott*" (I thank thee, gracious God). The sermon is a continuation of the Sunday service theme: *Dankbarkeit,* gratitude.

For the sermon text, the minister reads Deuteronomy 8:1 "Be careful to follow every command I am giving you today." Like most of our teachings, this evening's sermon originates from our ancestors' time in Europe: "Just as the Lord commanded the children of Israel to observe the Festival of Harvest, we too, should not come empty-handed," the minister says. "But we should honor God, acknowledge our dependence on him, and praise him for his rich blessings, both the spiritual and the material."

**7:00 p.m.** At the supper table, homemade pizza, applesauce, and fellowship with my communal family strike a familiar chord. Each time I sit here, I am reminded that we're not just here for "bread alone" but rather because "all the believers were together and had everything in common" (Acts 2:44).

I'm taken back to Süd Tirol, Italy, where one day during my Europe trip, I enjoyed pizza with some dear friends at a restaurant high in the mountains. All day we had been touring historical places, most of them connected with Jakob Hutter, elder of the Hutterites in the early 1500s. Feasting on local cuisine that evening was the exclamation mark for that memorable day. Following in the footsteps of our forebears, I came away with a deeper sense of gratitude for all they'd endured and for the blessings of living in Christian community today.

*9:30 p.m.* Long after the sun's splashes of splendid orange-gold have faded from the western sky, its reminder rings clear that "my cup overflows" (Psalm 23:5). May I never take my communal way of life for granted, nor the sacrifices of the brothers and sisters who have gone on before, leaving a lasting legacy of faithfulness.

As my days don't allow for enough time with books, I like to curl up with one before bedtime. Right now, I'm captivated by Duane C. S. Stoltzfus's *Pacifists in Chains: The Persecution of Hutterites during the Great War.* It's a story I know well, but the author has done a superb job of researching this part of our history. He includes numerous fascinating perspectives, thus enhancing this historic account and giving the reader a broader view of that era.

With the frog chorus echoing through my open window and lulling me to sleep, I'm convinced of carpe diem. The time is right to seize the day: to tuck my journals into one book and publish it.

# PART I

## *Fellowship*

# 1

# *Beehive Busyness*

*It was like the work of a clock where every cogwheel drives
another, and everything turns in an orderly way, or like a hive
of bees where all work together, some making wax, some making
honey, and some carrying nectar to the hive.*

—Hans Kräl, *Chronicle of the Hutterian Brethren*

**T**RUCKS ARE WAITING! Everybody welcome. Thank
you!" The crisp message sounds from the public address system, which can be heard in every home on our colony. Today
the message invites colony members to a shift of picking weeds
and lumps of dirt from newly harvested potatoes, traveling by
conveyor into the shed.

"This is a recorded announcement," one young woman dead-
pans. Grabbing gloves and a jacket, she heads for the potato
shed. "We can't allow McDonald's to run out of french fries!"

Every autumn brings the exciting racket of tractors, trucks,
and potato diggers rattling and rumbling their way to the potato
fields near our home on the prairies. Here three generations
gather to work on one project. Even the children eagerly help
to harvest the brown-skinned, white-fleshed Russet Burbank
potatoes, commonly used for french fries.

Harvest is one of the busiest times on a Hutterite colony. Most colonies raise a variety of crops, including wheat, oats, barley, canola, beans, and potatoes. At the peak of the season you can find one crew combining and another baling or swathing, with the field boss overseeing all of it. Every colony owns a number of combines, tractors, and grain wagons. During harvest, the wagons bring the grain from the combines to one of two waiting semitrucks, which in turn haul the grain to large bins on the colony.

While the men are busy in the fields, the women are in a flurry of activity in the kitchen. Here all meals are prepared for the entire community. During harvesttime there's extra work, as the men in the field get their meals brought to them. That way the entire crew doesn't have to stop their work to come home for lunch and supper, which would waste precious harvesttime. Some colonies have enough manpower and are able to work in shifts. Because our colony has a kitchen cabinet factory, however, this is not an option.

Once the grain is harvested, there are potatoes to dig. Some years, when the conditions are not favorable, combining takes longer. In those years the grain harvest overlaps into the potato harvest, making life extra busy.

Like farmers all over the globe, we put in long hours. It comes with the territory. Especially during potato harvest, hours are not dictated by a clock but by the tasks at hand, which can seem relentless.

For the most part, though, working together toward a common goal—harvesting, preparing meals, or any other chore—enhances the joy of our "all things common" journey (Acts 2:44). As the hymn says, "We shall come rejoicing, bringing in the sheaves."

Harvesting potatoes on Elm River Colony, where I live.

In the field, two John Deere tractors prepare to start, one pulling a four-row digger and the other a three-row digger. Jake, the potato manager, and his helper, Marvin, drive these massive machines slowly up and down the field. Each digger conveys the potatoes to a truck moving alongside, while the plants are returned to the field.

A fleet of four Ford trucks transports the potatoes to the concrete shed, where they are unloaded into a huge bin. With the capacity of about two tandem trucks of potatoes, the bin ensures an even flow of potatoes passing over the grading table on their way into storage. In dry conditions, a clodhopper is used to eliminate dirt clumps. In years that are too rainy, this machine cannot be used, as the wet earth would clog it.

At the grading table four people work quickly, taking out as much dirt as possible. Then, as the potatoes tumble onto a conveyor, the older children and adults continue the task. "Try to get all the dirt and small or green potatoes out," Mark, the foreman, instructs. "We don't want undue dockage at shipping time."

Finally the conveyor drops the spuds onto the hopper of the piler, which moves the potatoes into the shed. This huge telescopic, arm-like conveyor is remote controlled. It moves from side to side and up and down, creating a uniform pile that fills the shed to capacity.

The potato shed requires the most workers. Children, teenagers, fathers, mothers, grandfathers, and sometimes even grandmothers work along the conveyor. The result is a jovial atmosphere and tons of relatively clean potatoes in storage.

When my dad was still with us, he loved helping out at harvesttime as much as his job as chicken barn manager allowed. Working with so many brothers and sisters was a welcome break from his mostly solitary tasks. One of my favorite photos is of me working alongside dad at the potato conveyor. Sadly, it was also during potato harvest that he lost his battle with cancer.

One way to keep everybody in good spirits, even when tired and sore muscles beg for a break, is a healthy sense of humor. Sometimes that means citing facts that only farmers find fascinating. "Kevin, tell me once more," a young woman calls out, grinning. "How many orders of french fries does this shed hold?"

"For the last time: ninety thousand hundred-weight bags!" Kevin says. "Each bag yields five hundred orders of fries, about three ounces each. If you're good at mental math, you can figure it out quite easily. If not, the answer is forty-five million!"

One year, because of heavy rain, the star table, the section of the grading table that takes out most of the dirt and small potatoes, required more frequent cleaning. A young man climbed up and began unclogging it. Intent on finishing as quickly as possible, he didn't notice that a frayed piece of his coveralls

The star table, which helps remove dirt and small potatoes from the potato harvest.

snagged on the moving parts. Abruptly the machine grabbed the sleeve and ripped it off. Fortunately, someone close by pulled him away and stopped the machine before any serious harm occurred.

"Let this be a reminder for all of us to be more careful," a grandfather admonished. "It could have been much worse."

\* \* \*

When the shed is full, the door stays sealed to maintain a temperature of 9°C (48°F). From a pit under wooden floor slats, gigantic fans circulate air up through the potatoes. A humidifier ensures 98 percent humidity to prevent shrinkage. In this way, healthy potatoes can be stored from September to August of the following year without spoiling. After they are shipped, the shed is cleaned and disinfected in preparation for the next crop.

"An average crop yields about 365 bags per acre, and we've seen amounts close to 417," the potato manager explained to me one time. Yields fluctuate annually, depending on growing conditions. Potatoes thrive in cool weather, and cool nights are especially crucial.

Since potatoes are prone to disease, primarily blight, growers have to be vigilant. They must spray fungicide every eight days during dry conditions and every five days during wet conditions, starting when the plants are about thirty centimeters (twelve inches) high. When these measures fail, the only option is to watch the hard work and investment disappear under a plow. To prevent blight from spreading when there's only a touch of the disease, there's an expensive solution of spraying the potatoes as they go into the shed. "When you haul these potatoes to the processing plant," one farmer joked, "Don't stop for coffee. You simply can't afford it."

With good weather, our six hundred acres of potatoes can be harvested in approximately two weeks. Normally, digging begins around September 15, if it isn't too warm. The ideal temperature for digging is approximately 18°C (64°F): it is best that potatoes are cool upon storage. Poor weather can also prevent or delay potato harvest; then the risk is heavy frost damage.

"You girls at the grading table, let your hands move as fast as your mouth," Kevin hollers impatiently. "Do you want to be here till Christmas?"

In response, someone starts singing, "Oh, bring me a potato perogie" to the tune of "We Wish You a Merry Christmas." Kevin, clearly not in a festive mood, does not see the humor in this little ditty.

After a few weeks of long hours, weary bodies, and frayed nerves, when the potatoes are all in the shed, relief and gratitude

take over. Everyone enjoys a parade of trucks, tractors, and diggers returning to the colony from the field. We celebrate the end
of harvest with a barbeque supper of scrumptious baked potatoes with sour cream, and a tossed salad. After a cream cheese
dessert, everybody joins in singing a German evening hymn,
thankful for food on the table. More importantly, though, we're
grateful for the blessing of those with whom we live, work, and
celebrate, on the prairie of this land called Canada.

# 2

# *Beauty in the Ashes*

*The gem cannot be polished without friction,*
*nor man be perfected without trials.*

—Danish proverb

THE CARPENTRY SHOP is on fire!"

For a few seconds I wondered if this was a nightmare. Hearing the rest of my family rushing about, however, I knew it was all too real.

As we get carried away with our day-to-day activities, we hardly ever pause to ponder how quickly catastrophe can change our circumstances. This realization hit me one cool October night some years ago. A woman on our colony looked out her window at midnight and saw angry flames at the carpentry shop, our colony's flourishing furniture factory. I can still hear her strained, shaky voice over the colony public address system, which is connected to the homes on our colony. Minutes later most members of our colony were at the site, trying to extinguish the blaze or watching in disbelief as the building burned to a mound of metal and rubble.

Later when we discussed the tragedy, the woman who had alerted us to the fire told us how hard making this

The carpentry shop on the Elm River Colony in flames.

announcement was. She knew that seconds counted, and this knowledge was coupled with shock that made it hard to think straight. "What does one say at twelve o'clock at night, knowing one of our buildings is burning?" she recalled.

Twelve fire trucks—our own, some from our nearest town, Portage la Prairie, and others from Hutterite colonies in the area—surrounded the carpentry shop. They tried valiantly to douse the blaze, but shortly after they arrived, the building collapsed.

"We have nothing," one carpenter lamented later. "Not even screws or a tape measure!"

\*   \*   \*

Our furniture business, originally named Naturest Bedding, was established in 1991. It began in an old 40 x 28 ft. building, making waterbed and futon frames, bunk beds, dressers, and bedside tables. Since this was a relatively new and untried industry for a colony, the beginnings were hesitant and humble, with a steep learning curve. It soon became clear that this venture was not going to take off as hoped. So those involved in the business decided to target the kitchen cabinets and vanities market instead, under the name E & R Furnishings and Millwork.

These proved to be wise decisions. In a short time, to accommodate the growing number of orders, the carpenters and the colony leaders decided to expand. The shop moved into one side of the broiler barn, a relatively new 250 x 40 ft. building. But soon the venture needed even more room, so the whole building was utilized.

The larger building allowed the colony to invest in larger, more complex machinery: shapers, glue wheel, edge bander, and lathe and rip saws. "This meant we'd be able to expand our business and build furniture more efficiently," Irvin, the shop foreman, explained to me. For more than a decade, beautiful, sturdy cabinets were manufactured for private homes, hotels, doctors' offices, restaurants, and other businesses all over Manitoba and into Saskatchewan and Ontario. Our little shop was building a name as a quality furniture factory.

From Italy, our carpenters acquired a state-of-the-art Computer Numerically Controlled (CNC) router. It could cut, drill, and rout quickly and precisely. To accommodate the orders, the colony made plans to extend the building and add a CNC nesting machine for melamine, a durable, economic particle board, prefinished with a smooth laminate, used for the insides of cabinets.

Advertising was largely word of mouth, but sometimes our carpenters set up a booth at trade shows such as the Autumn Home Show in Winnipeg, Manitoba. This usually resulted in necessary exposure and, ultimately, kitchen cabinet orders.

Before the fire, E & R Furnishings employed seven full-time and four part-time workers. Now, with the building destroyed, what would happen? "I don't have a job after school," one high schooler said, his voice thick with emotion. "Carpentry is something I learned to enjoy. Now it's gone!"

* * *

Days after the fire, the carpenters talked about rebuilding. "No doubt, this is a severe setback," one of them said. "But I am confident we can rebuild and continue our business as strong as ever." A temporary shop was set up in a barn, and the office was located at the nursery school, which is used only during summer months. Contractors constructed a new 300 x 70 ft. building, and the colony ordered new machines.

Support from fellow Hutterites, as well as customers and various businesses, along with viable insurance, provided the means and determination to rebuild after this devastating loss. "We'll wait for our cabinets until you've rebuilt," some customers kindly offered. A machinery salesman provided three interest-free years on the purchase of new machines. And another colony promptly offered our carpenters space in their carpentry shop to build cabinets for the new houses being built at our colony at the time of the fire.

On the first Sunday after the fire, when this loss was still heavy on our minds, worshiping together with brothers and sisters was like a soothing balm. We were reminded of God's goodness, even in the face of tragedy. "Compared to all the things we still have to be thankful for, this building was but a speck," our minister reminded us. "We have every reason to lift our voices with the psalmist David, 'Praise the Lord, my soul, and forget not all his benefits'" (Psalm 103:2).

# 3

# Life Lessons from Grandpa

*Some of the world's best educators are grandparents.*
—Charles W. Shedd, American Presbyterian minister and author

IN HIS YOUNGER YEARS, Grandpa raised chickens. People still remember his work ethic and his matter-of-fact approach to farming and life in general. One time people who had grown up on our colony and who had left came back for a visit. As we walked around, listening to them reminisce, one man enthusiastically recalled, "I remember your grandpa in his old straw hat walking home from the barn. His clothes were always dusty. I thought he must be the most hardworking man on the colony!"

As children, my cousins and I sometimes helped him sweep the barn or bed down the baby chicks. Other times, helping Grandpa meant unloading the new baby chicks that had just arrived from Miller Hatcheries. The truck would park beside the old red barn, back toward the side wall, where a little door on the second level saved you from having to carry all the boxes up the stairs. While Grandpa knelt by the little door on the second floor, the truck driver stood on a straw-bale platform below and handed up the boxes to him, one by one. My cousins and I would then pick up the boxes and carefully tip each box, one at a time, to empty the chicks, according to my grandpa's instructions, "right under the brooder light." It didn't matter that in mere seconds those lively chicks would scatter all over their new pen.

"Why don't we unload all the boxes from the truck first before emptying any of them?" we suggested a few times. "That way the chicks wouldn't be underfoot while we're unloading the rest of them." I have vivid memories of the poor truck driver handing up the boxes to Grandpa, who was kneeling by the little door on the second level of the barn. After the few boxes had been emptied, the baby chicks always found that little door. This meant that, besides handing boxes to Grandpa, the driver had to catch wayward chicks. Some always managed to tumble down to the bales below.

Somehow this juggling act escaped Grandpa. Or rather, he didn't let it get in the way of his no-nonsense, I'm-in-charge-here attitude. That's just how you did it: end of story. We soon learned there was no point in trying to do it otherwise, much less argue our case. Still, we knew he meant well and always appreciated our help. Sometimes he'd even reward each of us with a piece of Bazooka bubble gum.

\* \* \*

After health issues forced him to give up raising chickens, Grandpa took up mowing lawns and repairing lawn mowers for colony families. For him, retiring to an easy chair was not an option. It soon became apparent to everybody that lawn mowers were his new babies. If you didn't want a stern lecture on how to take care of your mower, you did what he said. I was on the receiving end of quite a few of his impromptu lessons. They still ring in my ear whenever I go near a mower. It's as if Grandpa is admonishing me from his grave: "When was the last time you cleaned this machine properly?"

One year Stella, a girl from the Bruderhof, a Christian community in New York that was once affiliated with the Hutterites, came for a visit. While she was helping her host family with yard work, the lawn mower wouldn't start. She added more fuel, but it still didn't start. Having been with us for a while, Stella knew to take the mower to Grandpa to fix. With Stella watching, Grandpa tried to figure out what the problem was. After a few minutes he unscrewed the lid of the gas tank and stuck his stubby finger into it. As he'd by then suspected, it came out greasy.

"What did you put in here?" he asked brusquely.

"Well, it was out of gas, so I refilled it?" Stella answered, uncertain as to what she'd done wrong.

"Bring me the container of this 'gas' you put in here," Grandpa ordered, wiping his fingers on an old rag. Still confused, Stella hurried around the corner of the house to get the jug.

Grandpa raised the jug, looked at its dark, thick content, and tilted it back and forth slowly as if making a statement. "This is not gas! It is oil!" Grandpa lectured emphatically. "Don't New York girls know the difference between gas and oil? And I'll bet you went to college, too." At that time many Hutterites, especially those in the older generation, didn't see the value of education beyond grade eight. They firmly believed that all the schooling necessary could be gleaned from working alongside experienced adults, like Grandpa.

"This will take a while. No need for you to stand around here and watch," he continued. "I'll bring you the mower once it's cleaned and properly refueled!"

As he promised, Grandpa returned the mower after a few hours. It had been thoroughly cleaned and was running smoothly. But now, in big bold letters, a message on top of the gas tank read: GAS ONLY. Still perplexed by this mix-up, Grandpa instilled one more lesson as he walked away. "Oil is thick and dark and does not go in the gas tank!" he said, shaking his head.

Even though Grandpa sometimes came across as gruff and set in his ways, we all knew he had a heart as warm and soft as baby chicks. Spending time visiting with family and especially teasing his grandchildren brought him great joy. One of his frequent questions was, "What did you learn in school today?" To which we always answered, "Nothing."

"Then you have to go back tomorrow," he would inform us. We sometimes wondered: if we told him something we'd learned, would he have said we didn't have to go back?

\* \* \*

Grandpa loved playing jokes on people but never liked it when others played jokes on him. Because I'd inherited his always-good-for-laughs gene, however, I sometimes felt compelled to give him some of his own medicine. One year, during my teens, I decided to have some fun at Grandpa's expense.

At that time, Grandpa was still raising chickens. A few weeks before the chicks arrived, the hatchery would send out postcards to the buyers, informing them of the exact date on which to expect their new flock. Grandpa would wait for this all-important postcard as eagerly as the *Weinzedl,* the field manager, waited for the first signs of sprouting crops.

One early summer day, I found an old hatchery postcard that he had received a previous year. Grandpa was mowing our lawn with his riding mower when I casually walked up to him and handed him the supposed long-awaited postcard. He read it as he usually did: at arms-length to accommodate his failing eyesight. I held my breath, not daring to show any sign of mirth. "Is that man crazy?" he hollered after he read it. "In September! Two whole months I should wait for my chicks. I'm going to call him right now." He roared off, as fast as the little John Deere rider would carry him, forgetting our half-mown lawn.

For a few minutes, I stood rooted to the grass. When the realization hit me—the confusion my little prank would cause when he called the hatchery—I charged after him.

There was no stopping him, however. Muttering to himself the whole time, he was a man on a mission. I gave up the chase, wondering how to break this to my dad before he heard Grandpa's version. After some deliberation, I decided to let the proverbial chips fall where they may. I knew deep down that Dad would find this funny as well, but I also knew he'd want me to make things right with Grandpa.

Later that day, my aunt informed me that when Grandpa arrived home, he clearly had a bee under his old straw hat. Trying to be helpful, she asked what had him riled. He thrust the card at her. "I've never heard of having to wait months for baby chicks to arrive. The guy must be crazy!"

My aunt looked at the card and noticed the date, which was several years past. She pointed that out to him and asked, "Where did you get this card anyway?"

"Linda gave it to me," He answered. Scratching his head, he thought about that for a moment, the truth slowly dawning on him. "I'll have a chat with her dad about that one," he added, sternly. "No respect, those kids nowadays."

He must have been relieved that the late arrival of his chicks was just a joke, because he never did have that chat with my dad.

The next time Grandpa saw me, he shook his stubby finger at me. But the mischievous twinkle in his eyes told me all was forgiven. Eventually he may even have seen the humor in my card trick. After all, some family traits do get passed down from generation to generation. Like Grandma always said, "*Der Epfel follt nit weit vun Stom*" (The apple doesn't fall far from the tree).

# 4

# A Circle Not Unbroken

*There is a time for everything,*
*and a season for every activity under the heavens.*
—Ecclesiastes 3:1

ON A CRISP WINTER EVENING, my Night Writers group met, like we do every month, to critique and celebrate each other's work. One of my writing friends brought Patricia A. Williams's book *Once Upon a Lifetime,* and we passed it around. Full of ideas for recording events in one's life, this book appeared to be an excellent writer's tool, and I decided to try to obtain a copy. A page in my friend's copy provided the ordering information.

When I dialed the phone number, however, it led to an answering service with an empty promise: "Please leave your name and number, and we'll call you as soon as possible." The Web address drew a blank, and the email address was a virtual boomerang.

At $19.95, the book was reasonably priced—if only I could find someone to take my money! But somebody clearly forgot to tell online booksellers what this book is worth. At that time, they offered used copies for $181.31. As much as I wanted it, sacrificing a year's worth of coffee and chocolate wasn't an option. Five stores in Winnipeg informed me the book was out of print.

Now that electronic connections give us information at our fingertips, I decided to try some e-magic. I Googled the book's name until I felt my eyes cross, with no magic in sight. The information highway left me wondering why I was so driven to find this book.

Finally, I found an online review of the book by a John Melchinger. It was a long shot, but I fired off an email to him asking if he knew where I could get a copy of this book. He replied that he might have some copies, and perhaps an audio version as well, but he would have to check first. He told me that he also happened to know the author very well. Touchdown! I now knew I'd get a copy of the book.

The story continued to unfold, however, like something from *Chicken Soup for the Soul*. In fact, it gave the phrase "Once upon a lifetime" a whole new meaning. Upon learning that I live in Manitoba, John Melchinger informed me, "My wife, Jayne, is originally from Oakville, Manitoba. We make our home in Tampa, Florida, now."

Living in the Oakville area, I was naturally curious. So I replied: "Small world! I live on a Hutterite colony just five miles from Oakville. Perhaps we know Jayne's family."

John wrote back: "My wife, Jayne Alford-Melchinger, is the younger sister of Bette Holliday, who still lives in Oakville. Their mother used to teach at a nearby Hutterite colony."

My family had known the Alfords in Oakville, but we had lost touch over the years when some of the family died and others moved away. But I wondered if my kindergarten teacher, Mrs. Audrey Alford, might happen to be Jayne's mother.

"Audrey Alford was indeed Jayne's mother," John wrote. "She taught at your colony from 1968 to 1970. Jayne said one of those Christmas Eves a Hutterite family's home burned down and she donated her favorite dolly to a little girl. Small world indeed."

John's answer took me back to a tragic time for my family. Yes, it is a small world, and he didn't even know how small when he sent that email. The time of the fire was not quite accurate, but that detail wasn't so important. The multi-family house fire happened on an extremely cold January evening. Nobody ever learned how it had started. The fire affected me more deeply than John knew; it took the lives of my two little brothers and left my sister with severe burns. She had to be hospitalized for many months. I was at the children's dining room having supper, so I was not hurt.

At five years of age, I was also too young to have a real sense of this loss and what it meant for my family and the other families who lost their home. One thing I clearly remember from that tragic day is that, while the house was still in flames, my friends asked me to come to their house, as it was too cold to stay outside for long. There one of the girls suggested we pray. So a circle of little girls knelt down on that hardwood floor, near the coal stove in the living room, and prayed. We asked God to help us and ended our petition with the Lord's Prayer.

Dad, Mom, and I lived at my grandparents' house until another home was built. That part was comforting. In addition to Grandma and Grandpa, there were five aunts there to dote on me, especially since my parents had to spend a lot of time with my sister at the hospital.

I was in grade one at the time. And as you may have guessed by now, I was the little girl to whom Jayne gave her favorite dolly. I remember it well; tall with dark hair, which I always fondly called *ma Alford Puppela* (my Alford doll).

In the end, John Melchinger generously sent me a copy of the book that had taken me on an interesting and emotional virtual ride. Then, after many years, against obvious odds and thanks to an electronic connection, I was able to thank Jayne for her noble gift. That doll meant so much to me in those sad days, for I had not only lost all my toys but also my home and, worst of all, my two brothers.

As John so eloquently put it: "All of life seems an endless array and disarray of circles that cross every which way. This circle is not broken, although the way it came around to be whole is quite amazing."

# 5

# Trotting on Trust

*The art of communication is the language of leadership.*
—James Humes, American author and presidential speechwriter

**W**HEN MY COLONY, Elm River, was established in 1935, colony members relied on machines that ran on oats to farm the land. In his younger days, my dad loved working with these "tractors"—horses, of course—and occasionally helped break wild ones. I grew up hearing countless horse tales. Thus began my fascination with these magnificent animals. I especially enjoy watching humans and horses doing extraordinary things in tandem.

While horses played a huge role on early Manitoba Hutterite colonies, today they're used mostly for leisure activities. Some Hutterites, however, take such leisure to a whole new level. People like my second cousin Judith prove that with the proper mix of psychology, principles, practice, and patience, a phenomenal human-horse partnership can emerge.

When I heard about Judith and her horses, I was chomping at the bit to write about it. I started emailing with Judith to learn about horsemanship as taught by the Parelli Program, in which Judith had been trained. This program teaches people how to

Judith and her horse, Tess.

communicate, through body language, in a way that the horse understands. The founder, Pat Parelli, believes the program helps horse lovers achieve "success without force, partnership without dominance, teamwork without fear, willingness without intimidation and harmony without coercion."

With each email from Judith, it became clearer to me how passionate she is about her hobby. Watching her communicating with horses, you get a good sense of the beautiful relationship between her and her horse. "It's not so much the things I do with horses," Judith says; it's about "the psychology and principles behind it all."

I watched a video in which Judith and her horse, Tess, go into some water. I'd never seen a horse patiently wait in deep water until its rider gets back from an impromptu plunge. "Horses frequently panic when getting into water and also when facing dangers," Judith told me. "Those traits are what helped them survive as a species." In one email, she went on to explain:

I often tell children that horses are big, four-legged chickens, so getting Tess to trust my leadership enough to go into the water is huge. There are a couple reasons why that is true. First, horses can't see potential predators in the water, and trust me: some horses really believe there is an alligator hiding in a one-inch-deep puddle. Secondly, horses' feet are their main means of escape from predators either by running, kicking, or striking. Once they are in the water, that power is taken away from them, putting them in a very vulnerable position.

Getting Tess to go in the water and stay there until further notice is all about trusting me, her leader. And that trust comes from having a relationship that was established through love, language, and leadership in equal doses. The love is the easy part, the language needs to be one that she understands, and the leadership requires a competent leader. Everything I do with Tess all boils down to how good my relationship is with her.

As the leader, I need to be able to tell if Tess is refusing to go in the water because she's afraid or refusing because she's being defiant and testing my leadership. As her leader, it's imperative to make that distinction. If I force Tess to go in the water when she's afraid, I lose her rapport, respect, and trust, and have a mental wreck on my hands.

However, if I realize that she's afraid and take my time to build her confidence, that will build on her level of respect and trust in me as her leader as well. This will result in a happier, more confident, and willing horse who wants to be with me. Similar to humans, a horse will jump higher and run faster out of heart and desire as opposed to being forced into doing something. Now Tess loves the water, especially on hot summer days!

Judith playing with her horse.

When Judith first started working with horses, some Hutterite people were skeptical, perhaps because the Parelli method was new to them and they were uncertain whether it was something with which Hutterites should be involved. Change is not always easy. Being a trailblazer, however, Judith persevered. She has found more and more opportunities to use her passion and knowledge of horses to help humans. Judith, who is also a nurse, is now a facilitator in a Kids Can Cope program; through horses, she and others help children cope when family members are sick with cancer. Judith also teaches horsemanship and riding to the children at her colony and occasionally at a local Bible camp. She also helps other people with their horses and gives countless visitors to her colony a positive experience with horses.

Listening to Judith, I came away thinking, *Principles of horsemanship apply to our relationships with fellow humans as well!* Clear and open communication is important if we wish to maintain healthy, happy relationships. This is especially true in the communal life we practice, where we rub shoulders with our neighbour on a daily basis. Relationships get strained when admonitions are taken negatively, or when idiosyncrasies and rude behaviors rankle like nails on a chalkboard. Other times unclear and unhealthy communication can make loving your neighbor a little challenging. For the most part, we don't intentionally give our neighbor a hard time. Still, something as simple as our body language or the way we greet someone can hurt others' feelings. As a friend of mine aptly stated, "On a colony the wolf and the sheep have to learn to get along." Sometimes we simply come across as the wolf; other times we are more like the sheep.

The lessons that Judith has learned look a lot like the lesson in 1 Corinthians 13:4-7: "Love is patient, love is kind. It does not envy, it does not boast, it is not proud. It does not dishonor others, it is not self-seeking, it is not easily angered, it keeps no record of wrongs. Love does not delight in evil but rejoices with the truth. It always protects, always trusts, always hopes, and always perseveres."

We haven't had horses on our colony for many years. If the number of children who walk around our colony wearing cowboy hats is any indication, however, horses would be well received. I'm hoping one day our little cowgirls and cowboys can have this dream realized and write their own chapter of history with horses. When that day comes, I hope they'll have someone like Judith to teach them about trotting on trust.

# 6

# To Write a Hutterite Story

*The dreams and passions stored within hearts*
*are powerful keys which can unlock a wealth of potential.*
—John C. Maxwell, American author, speaker, and pastor

LINDA, DO IT! We *need* stories about different cultures; that's one way of learning about each other!"

These inspiring words from Myrelene Ranville, an author and friend from Canada's Aboriginal Anishinaabe community, were exactly what I needed to propel me from dreaming about my story to actually writing it. In late fall 2004, Myrelene visited our school and brought her children's book, *Tex*. After she read us her story, we sat down to enjoy coffee and cake and to hear how her book has taken her to many interesting places, including Europe. That's when I shared my dream of one day publishing a German children's book. Myrelene got very excited and encouraged me to do it. In the winter of that school year, I started the first draft of my story.

For many years, writing has been one of my favorite activities. In addition to the joy of being creative with language and feeling the fulfillment a completed piece of work brings, I find it incredibly relaxing. While other Hutterite women love to sew, I would rather write. It's not something I have in common with many of my fellow Hutterites, but I'm fine with that. We have so many things in common that it's okay to differ in some areas. Just as each individual flower adds its distinct loveliness to the garden, so our various talents and strengths bring richness and beauty to our community.

Thinking back to my school days, I realize that my non-Hutterite English teachers never encouraged me to write about my own life. The rare occasions when I did creative writing, I produced fictitious tales that lacked feeling—adaptations of things I'd read in books. Nothing in them resembled what I knew and loved: my own Hutterite community. I've loved to write ever since I learned how, but I could never get into writing made-up stories. Back then, my best writing happened in letters to pen pals and relatives.

I'm not sure why our teachers didn't suggest we write about our own Hutterite lives. I can't imagine that anyone would feel that there's nothing interesting to say about it. Today, however, the students in our school write mostly about experiences from their own lives, and they proudly publish many of these pieces in our school newspaper. I make sure my students know that their Hutterite stories are worth writing about, because they are interesting, heartwarming, and valuable—just like many of the stories that they read.

As any writer knows, drafting and revising require many hours of diligent labor. It was no different when I was writing my first book, *Lindas glücklicher Tag*, which translates as *Linda's Happy Day*. Several people edited it for me, which always meant revising yet again. One of the editors, Karli Suess, a former German language consultant here in Manitoba, suggested I write all the dialogue in our Carinthian German dialect. Originating in the province of Kärnten, Austria, we fondly call the dialect Hutterisch.

"Karli!" I responded incredulously. "You know Hutterisch is a dialect and has no written form!"

Not to be deterred, he calmly replied, "Then change that!" I was not convinced that this idea had any merit; I'd have to invent a Hutterisch written form. Even after trying to change the dialogue on a few pages, I was still extremely hesitant. Writing the language I spoke every day felt strange, and seeing the words in print was simply weird.

In some ways it was also wonderful. I'd never seen so much Hutterisch used in a story before, and the local color added something very personal. I eventually decided to go with Karli's suggestion. Much later, I realized that it lent authenticity to my story. Adding Hutterisch made this part of the editing process a learning experience in itself. However, with each revision the story got better until I had a beautiful piece of work that was uniquely Hutterite in content, illustrations, and language.

Finishing my story came at an opportune time. The Hutterian Brethren Book Centre, a small Manitoba book supplier was exploring the possibility of publishing its own books. The manager, who would also be in charge of the publishing, asked me if they could publish my story, which my sister Sonia had begun to illustrate. He had heard about it through a friend and colleague who was one of the editors. I rejoiced in my good fortune at not having to search for a publisher!

*Lindas glücklicher Tag* was launched in August 2006, at the International Hutterian Educators' Conference in Portage la

erzählt von **Linda Maendel**
mit Bildern von **Sonia Maendel**

## Lindas glücklicher Tag

*Lindas glücklicher Tag*, the first children's book published with Hutterisch text.

Prairie, Manitoba. The launch was an exciting historical event not only for me but for all Hutterites: this was the first published children's book to be both written and illustrated by Hutterites! Finally our children would be able to open a book and identify with the people, the language, and culture in the story. Since its publication, a number of English, German, and even Hutterisch children's books are gracing our library shelves—written by Hutterites, for Hutterites, and for anybody else who's interested.

Today, children in many Hutterite colonies and people who visit our local library enjoy *Lindas glücklicher Tag*. The writer in me also never stops dreaming. I'm still dreaming of finding a market in German-speaking countries and publishing more books in the future.

When my copies arrived from the publisher, I held those shiny wonders in my hand and breathed in the smell of ink on new paper. *What would Dad say if he could see my published book?* I wondered. An avid reader and storyteller himself, he helped instill in me the love of literacy. He never articulated the significance of reading and sharing stories, but growing up, I saw how much he relished every opportunity to relate some personal experience or account he'd read.

While Dad told his stories to family and friends, I share mine in books, my blog, and newspaper articles. I'm grateful for the timeless gift of story; it is yet another way to be close to my dad in spirit. I'm also grateful that I can pass on to children the skill of writing and sharing their unique and beautiful experiences. I hope my example will light a fire that will motivate them to keep writing and hopefully one day to publish their stories.

# 7

# Two Empty Chairs

*Some of us think holding on makes us strong;*
*but sometimes it is letting go.*

—Hermann Hesse, German-Swiss writer and poet

COMING TO SCHOOL THAT SPRING DAY was not like every other day, with happy children chattering in the hallway. The children weren't as chipper as usual. The sad event of the day before had left a dark cloud hanging over us. Two of our young students moved away from the only life they'd ever known, after their parents made the decision to leave the colony for another province.

People in mainstream society move all the time; it is part of life. When you live on a Hutterite colony and decide to leave, especially as an entire family, the community life is disrupted.

When a Hutterite child is born, the whole community rejoices. That child is cared for not only by his or her family but by the whole community. He or she will most likely have a baby-sitter, who may or may not be a family member. At two and a half years of age, children enter *Klanaschuel*, a summer nursery run by mothers of the community. It is here where children are introduced to being in a group away from their families, and where *Gmanschoft* (community) is instilled through singing, praying, playing, napping, eating together, and sharing with others the toys, swings, and their caregivers' time.

Five is a special age; it's then that Hutterite children start eating in the *Essenschuel* (children's dining room), supervised by the German teacher and his wife. That's where they will eat most meals until the end of childhood. When they turn fifteen, they are considered adults; they will eat with all the other adults, join the workforce, and contribute to the community wherever needed.

When they enter school, most Hutterite children have non-Hutterite teachers, hired by the secular school divisions. However, many are blessed to have a Hutterite teacher as well. Besides nurturing the children intellectually, schools located on the colonies offer excellent opportunities to learn about Christian community, values, and beliefs from brothers and sisters who understand and appreciate the Hutterite culture and way of life.

When children play on the colony, adults are always nearby, looking out for them. The same is true when they help with various chores or run errands. From a young age children are encouraged to help with various chores: helping Mom around the house and kitchen, or working alongside Dad and learning about things like farming and taking care of animals. At times there are communal projects like cleaning the colony in spring, which includes raking leaves and clearing ditches and shrubs of debris.

From the cradle to the grave, Hutterites are cared for and loved by their own people. Through celebrations, sorrows, daily ordinary activities, and everything in between, Hutterites relish being together. Thus, when someone decides to leave, it is an extremely sad time for the whole community.

It's not uncommon for individuals and even families to leave their Hutterite way of life. People leave for a variety of reasons. Some join other churches, while others leave their life of faith altogether. Many are looking to experience a different lifestyle or want to try living on their own, away from the shelter of their community.

Even though we don't advocate staying if the heart is somewhere else, this does not lessen the pain when people choose to leave. We're together on a daily basis: we worship, work, eat, play, travel, learn, relax, and visit in big or small groups, year in, year out. Therefore, when someone forsakes the colony, they leave an ache that is unlike any other—and hard to explain to non-Hutterites.

I thought the last day these two dear students were here was going to be the hardest. It wasn't. The day after they left was much worse. I felt like sitting in their empty chairs and crying. I tried to picture them in a big-town school and how much of a culture shock that would be. There will be a mountain of adjustments for the whole family. Tears began to flow. I was at a loss for how to offer meaningful words of comfort to a little girl whom I found standing beside her friend's cubby hole, wiping away tears and saying, "I just wish she wouldn't have moved away."

Still, life marches on and things get easier, for us and most likely for them as well. The chairs are no longer empty, but there's a spot in our hearts that is. I wish this family well in their new life, and I look forward to the time when they'll come for visits.

# PART II

## Celebrations

# 8

# Marriages Strengthened by Community

*One and one makes one in the bond of marriage.*
*One and one makes one forever.*
*What a perfect plan for a man and woman,*
*joined in love by God's own hand.*

—George Wipf, Hutterite teacher and songwriter

**W**ELCOME TO YOUR NEW HOME! We have forty long rows of peas waiting to be picked early next week!" Thus reads one of the amusing signs welcoming one Hutterite bride to her new home.

Traditionally, a Hutterite bride moves to the colony of her husband-to-be—unless, of course, she already lives there, which is sometimes the case. Most often the bride is from another colony, which means the bridegroom travels to that colony on Saturday, where an evening farewell meal will take place. The groom brings his bride to his home colony early on the Sunday morning of the wedding. The guests arrive at the same time, and all are met about half a mile from the colony by a group we

call "the welcoming committee." This usually includes a decorated tractor and trailer with cheering children. This entourage
can be ten vehicles long, including a van or pickup truck pulling a trailer with the bride's belongings. Along this route there
may be signs with amusing messages for the bride, hinting at
what she can look forward to.

The bridal procession makes its way around the colony and
then parks where the couple and the guests will be greeted by
community members. Sometimes this is the first glimpse members of the groom's colony get of the bride, as the two colonies
may not have had a lot of contact before. A wedding usually
changes that. Not only are two families brought together, but the
two colonies also become bonded in a new way. This increased
fellowship sometimes leads to one or more other marriages.

The couple receives wedding gifts from their families and
also from relatives and friends of other colonies. The groom's
colony provides a home and furnishings for the couple.
Sometimes this is a trailer home or one of the colony-built
homes. If neither of these are available at the time, the couple
lives in the home of the groom's parents temporarily. A cousin
of mine enjoyed this arrangement. "We had such wonderful
times together," she said, "and they really helped me get accustomed to my new home."

On their wedding day, Hutterite brides usually wear blue
dresses, while grooms always wear black suits, often made by a
family member, and a white or pale colored shirt. Unlike bridal
dresses of mainstream society, Hutterite wedding dresses are of
the same pattern used for every other dress. However, on her
wedding day, the bride's jacket is of the same fabric as the rest
of her dress, rather than the usual black. Some claim the blue

wedding dress tradition started when the Hutterites arrived in America in late 1800s. During those early years, the Hutterites came into contact with the Amana Colonies, another immigrant religious community, who helped them financially and sold them, among other things, "Amana blue" fabric.

The wedding ceremony takes place at nine thirty in the morning. The service begins with a German wedding song such as "*Preiset mit mir den Herren*," a selection from our *Songs of Our Forefathers* book. The teaching is from Ephesians 5:22-33, with an exhortation to keep Christ as the center of a marriage. For the entire service the bride and groom sit with the others in attendance in our usual arrangement for worship: women and men on separate sides. However, two pews are reserved—one for the bride, her sisters, and other relatives, and one for the groom and members of his family, directly across the aisle from the bride.

After the sermon the bridal pair is asked to come to the front, where the wedding vows are exchanged. There is no ring exchange at the ceremony, although some couples do wear rings. After the vows, the minister then blesses the marriage with these words:

> Finally, together with the whole church, we wish for you the blessing of the Almighty, eternal God—yes, the God of Abraham, Isaac, and Jacob. May he join you together and fulfill his blessing in you, that you may dwell together as an upright and godly married couple, live together peacefully, and serve God as long as you live. We wish you this once more from God, through Jesus Christ. Amen.

The meals and snacks at a Hutterite wedding are prepared by the women of the host colony and served by *die Buebm*, the

Wedding cake made by Sonia Maendel, my sister.

young men. These same *Buebm* help the women with cleanup after the meal.

The noon meal consists of *Geastel* soup, beef brisket, horse-radish, steamed vegetables, a salad plate, and a cream-cheese dessert. *Geastel* is a crumbly flour-and-eggs mixture, which, after it has been air-dried, is added to broth, seasoned with chicken soup base, and cooked for a few minutes. Before it's served, the soup is often gar-nished with parsley. One time a guest from Austria attended a Hutterite wedding. When she noticed what was being served, she pointed out, "Only Hutterites and people in Carinthia, Austria, serve *Geastel* soup, beef brisket, and horseradish at a wedding. After all these centuries, some of your meals can still be traced back to your European roots!"

The wedding cake is usually made by someone from the colony, although sometimes they ask someone from another colony to do it. For many years, my sister Sonia has been deco-rating wedding cakes for couples married at our colony. Each guest receives a box of chocolates, along with a piece of white tea cake specially baked in a small tinfoil container

One particularly wet year, the communal dining room where we gathered at three o'clock for an afternoon of singing and snacks was fittingly decorated with a Noah's Ark theme. The two-by-two thing, coupled with the fact that we were having a wet year, seemed to be a fitting theme. That time we had six adult and children's choirs, a men's quartet, a duet, and some recitations and skits by the children. Near the beginning of the reception, I heard one of my favorite songs, "You Raise Me Up," sung beautifully by one of the visiting choirs.

The supper menu is generally lighter than the lunch menu. It may include mushroom soup, cold cuts, fresh homemade buns, salad, and a fruit platter with dip for dessert.

At one recent wedding, another highlight came near the end of the day, when someone requested that our choir and two guest choirs sing "Pilot Me." This has become somewhat of a tradition, not only for weddings but other events as well. It was a fitting way to end a wonderful *Huchzeit* (wedding) celebration. Even though this is not a wedding song, it's still fitting, especially for the bride.

Besides getting accustomed to a colony of new people, the bride will also have to adjust to the way things are done in her new home, which can be drastically different from what she's used to. For some, giving up familiar surroundings and trying to fit into the new can be difficult. Eventually, though, after strange has melted into normal, most new Hutterite wives can proudly proclaim, "It's like I've always been here."

# 9

# Christmas on the Colony

*He who has not Christmas in his heart*
*will never find it under a tree.*
—Roy L. Smith, American clergyman and author

LIVING ON A HUTTERITE COLONY, we are accustomed
to spirited debates among the men and boys about the merits
of a certain line of farm equipment or vehicle. One day, I overheard a group of them. "That new John Deere 8320 gives us
no trouble at all," one man boasted. "Whatever the task, it just
keeps humming along, eh?"

"You're never going to see this place without Ford and John
Deere!" said another. The others, including the boys whose eyes
shone with wonder at the glowing report of their favorite tractors, nodded their agreement.

In school some time later, I bent over Kris, who was having
trouble sorting objects with a Venn diagram. Intent on explain-
ing what to do, I saw the futility of my task when I realized that
Kris's mind was somewhere else entirely. "Have you seen our
new Ford truck?" he asked dreamily.

A few days before Christmas the teachers and students
enjoyed a delicious supper of pizza, tossed salad, and Saskatoon

cream cheese dessert. Before opening gifts, the children enthusiastically sang Christmas carols, beginning with the German version of *O Christmas Tree*.

*O Tannenbaum, O Tannenbaum* (O Christmas tree, O Christmas tree),

*Wie treu sind deine Blätter* (How lovely are thy branches)!

Watching the children open their Christmas gifts was a delightful experience. Overwhelmed with excitement, they forgot about the all-important brand name! Christmas wrapping colored the floor and children elatedly showed off shiny new toys.

"Wow! A remote-controlled pickup!" exclaimed Kris. "Just what I wanted!" He compared his Chevy truck with his friend Adrian's, and they were as exuberant as only tractors and trucks could make them.

"Apparently, if it makes tractor noise, has blinking lights, or moves at the touch of a button, nothing else matters," I told another teacher, relieved. "I guess it's not the brand name that runs the engine after all."

A few days later, Kris was playing with his brand new truck when it broke down. "Michael, can you fix my broken truck?" he asked his older brother.

Eventually, his dad took a look. Finally, he said, "Sorry, Kris, I can't see what's wrong with it." Patting Kris's head consolingly, he added, "I'll return it to the store. Perhaps they'll exchange it."

Exasperated and dejected, Kris tucked his truck under his arm and walked away. "If it were a Ford, I'm sure it would still be running!" he muttered.

\* \* \*

We started Christmas concert practice in late November, and everybody worked diligently to learn their pieces. One grade-three boy, Jonathan, needed extra help with one word. In our German recitation of "The Four Candles," Jonathan had a line from Romans 15:13 (KJV): "*Gott aber der Hoffnung erfülle euch mit aller Freude und Frieden im Glauben*" (Now the God of hope fill you with all joy and peace in believing).

Jonathan struggled daily with articulation, and he simply could not remember the word *Freude* (joy). Instead, he always said *Freunde* (friends). While God does indeed give us *Freunde*, we told him, in this verse it just wouldn't make sense. Jonathan had no problem saying *Freude* in isolation, but when he said his line, he simply could not get it right.

Teachers, parents, siblings, and fellow students tried to help him, but alas, nothing worked. On our last day of practice, I resigned myself to the fact that he would never get it. I just hoped the audience would be able to figure out what he was saying.

On the night of our program, Jonathan looked sharp, dressed in his Sunday best: pale green shirt and black pants. Standing on stage with the other students, he was beaming, as if he had not a care in the world. I was sitting in the front row in case the students needed prompts. I kept telling myself not to worry about Jonathan's almost certain mix-up. His was the last line of the piece, and everybody else had done their parts well.

While I was still wondering whether it would help him if I mouthed the word, Jonathan eagerly started his verse. All of us who had worked with him held our breaths . . . and then sighed with relief when he said the word perfectly. His bright smile said it all; he was happier about this accomplishment than any of us!

Later, when we reflected on our Christmas program, *Freude* took on a whole new meaning for Jonathan and for all of us. Jonathan told us how happy he was that he was finally able to say his piece flawlessly. When asked how he did it, he simply replied, "I asked God to whisper it in my ear, and he did." I was reminded of God's promise in Matthew 7:7: "Ask, and it will be given to you."

*     *     *

"Write about what makes your community special," the contest rules read. I forget where I saw this, but the thought stuck in my head like a bow on a gift. It was not so much because I contemplated entering the contest, but more because it made me think. What *is* it that makes my community special? Because there are more reasons than strands of tinsel on a Christmas tree, picking the special ones is difficult to determine. It took tiny voices to help me focus on some of them.

It has become a Christmas tradition for the mothers of our colony to go on a three-day shopping trip. Sometimes this takes them to shopping centers in Grand Forks, North Dakota. With so many mothers gone at the same time, those stoking the home fires happily fill in for them. In the children's dining room, the German teacher has someone other than his wife helping him supervise the children during meals. Babysitters replace moms. With the three regular cooks gone, three others replace them. The dishwashing rotation becomes a mix taken from the four regular shifts. "Which dish-wash group is it, anyway?" a woman once joked. "It's like fruit basket upset!"

With his mom and grandma gone, one kindergartner came to school all day instead of just for the morning. In many ways, the absence of the mothers for these few days makes the colony feel like a Christmas tree without lights.

Now, as I contemplated the childish chatter of six kindergarten students during their midmorning break, my heart was especially warm. Before eating their snack, one of them said grace. After the prayer was finished, Joel promptly announced, "Yesterday evening I prayed that the moms come home safely." A lump the size of a fruit drop cookie lodged in my throat. Instilled in this five-year-old was a strong sense of community: not only had he learned to pray for the protection of his own mommy but for that of other mommies as well.

Another little voice had me quickly swallowing the lump in my throat so that I could answer. "Linda, is my mom coming home today?" Evelynne asked with imploring blue eyes. "I cried for her last night."

"Yes," I assured her. "They should be here at suppertime." With a face twinkling like a Christmas light, she returned to her snack.

At home after school, listening to Christmas music while working on my laptop, I heard a chipper voice ring through the public address system. "The shoppers have crossed the border and should be here around seven o'clock." As the last strains from "I'll Be Home with Bells On" faded away on my CD player, I smiled, thinking of my students.

A few hours later, family and friends watched from the snow-packed parking lot as the bus rolled into our colony. With quiet gratitude I took in a joyous scene of squealing children dancing around their dads. As the moms stepped from the bus they were engulfed by smiles, cheers, and hugs. Another fruit drop cookie lodged in my throat. I had my answer: this was one example of what was special about my community.

This sentiment holds true as we observe our Christmas holy days. Besides family and school events, Hutterites observe Christmas with three morning church services. On December 25 we hear the New Testament story of Jesus' birth from Luke's gospel. This is followed by teachings on love, faith, and eternal life from John 3:16 on December 26.

The next day, a teaching about the Old Testament prophecies explains the Messiah's effect on people. The minister emphasizes the joy and gratitude we owe for the miracle that made it possible for us to live in Christian community as sisters and brothers. He also exhorts us to maintain forgiving spirits and be willing to share and serve the community wherever we can.

There's also a lot of singing of German and traditional English Christmas songs, both communally and in family settings. Each community has adult and children's choirs that sing for the festive Christmas meals, when the whole community eats together in the adults' dining hall. Christmas Eve, however, is the time when families gather individually to sing, share gifts, and enjoy snacks.

Though Dad is no longer with us, each Christmas we still hear his gentle reminder: "Christmas is much more than giving and receiving gifts."

# 10

# *Sisterly Love—*
# *Laced with Revenge*

*Sometimes life gives us lessons sent in ridiculous packaging.*
—Dar Williams, American singer-songwriter

**H**OW DOES THIS BRAT get away with opening his present now?" I complained a few days before Christmas many years ago. "And the rest of us have to wait till Christmas Eve!"

"He's only five and doesn't understand," Mom answered, clearly not bothered about this latest stunt. "Maybe next time you shouldn't tell him which gift is his."

The object of my rage was oblivious to my tirade. James, the baby in our family, was already happily playing with his Christmas present: a semitrailer car carrier. A few minutes before, alone in the living room, he had cozied up to the Christmas tree, where all the gifts had been waiting for weeks. Before we knew it, he had torn away the wrapping, revealing his dream toy.

Five years old or not, he shouldn't have done it. I was incensed that Mom wasn't on my side. "Well, do something!" I wailed. "Take it away from him. Hide it where he won't find it. And why does he always get away with stuff like this?"

"Just look how cute he is playing with his truck," Mom cooed. Then, switching from Hutterisch to English so James wouldn't understand, she continued, "After a while he will leave it and I will put it away. Why make him cry now?"

Living on a Hutterite colony, our family speaks Hutterisch, a German dialect. It's common practice to resort to English when parents or older siblings don't want little children to know what they're saying. "No, Mom, this is not cute!" I retorted in Hutterisch, unwilling to let this go and feeling no need to use English either.

Just then Dad arrived, and I took my case to him. "James opened his present. And Mom isn't doing anything about it," I stated in my best big-sister voice.

"Little boys can." Dad answered nonchalantly, hanging his coat and fur cap on the rack beside the door.

*Great! I should have known,* I thought. *The usual response; as steady as the clock chiming the hour. As if being the baby came with special privileges! Dad's "little boys can" supposedly makes everything all right.*

I strutted to my bedroom like a rooster who had just lost a few feathers in a fight but refused to admit defeat. *Fine! I'll put an end to this myself. Little boys can! Just wait and see. Big sisters* can *too!*

When my sister Elma came home I shared my dilemma, desperate to drum up support. "What will we do?" Elma asked, fully agreeing that we had to step in.

"Mom will probably rewrap the truck tonight after that brat is in bed," I fumed. "We have to do something with that gift. I'm sick of his stunts."

"And what can you do that Mom and Dad wouldn't notice?" Elma wanted to know.

"First we'll have to find a box about the same size as James's gift. We'll put something in it and wrap it with the same paper." I knew that it would not be a problem to find the same paper. Mom, always thrifty, bought a giant roll of wrapping paper a few years ago. To stretch it over more yuletide seasons, every Christmas Eve she would carefully cut the tape with a sharp knife before handing us gifts to unwrap. While we marveled over our newest treasures, Mom would fold the wrapping and stack it neatly on the floor beside her. This ritual was as much a part of our Christmas as roast duck and sauerkraut. And for that Christmas anyway, Mom's thriftiness was going to be the "plum pudding" that would help make this holiday memorable.

"I'll go to the attic to see if I can find a box and something to put in it," Elma offered the next day, obviously still pleased to be part of the plan. "You sneak to Mom's closet to see if you can find the wrapping paper. And leave everything the way you found it."

Before long we were in our bedroom, all set to start on our plum pudding plan. Thankfully, Mom had gone to Grandma's house with our younger siblings and Dad was at the hatchery, where he was getting ready for the upcoming hatching season.

Elma found the perfect box and an even more perfect gift to tuck inside. "I just want to see his face when he opens this!" I exclaimed as we wrapped the gift, my fury now replaced by glee.

"Me too," Elma chuckled. "One glimpse at this dilly and our lesson will make him wish he never heard 'little boys can.'"

By the time the rest of the family got home, we had switched the gifts, hiding the real one in our closet. We tried to look as angelic as the cherub on top of the tree, hoping to keep our secret under our bonnets until Christmas Eve.

A few days later, envisioning his truck, our bratty brother raced around the room excitedly, hugging our gift, still unwrapped. But moments after Mom cut the tape and he saw what it was, he sent our offering sailing across the room.

A scraggly-haired old doll, minus a few limbs, landed in a corner. Even Mom and Dad smiled. Then they quickly ordered us to get the other gift.

Years have a way of changing our outlook. In the eyes of a fourteen-year-old big sister, the broken doll was well deserved. Since then, I've concluded that I was the one who learned the most valuable lesson that day. Mom and Dad were right: sometimes letting things go works best.

Today my brother has two young sons, and I see that his payback will be sweeter than anything I could have dished out. At times I have to chuckle, or even laugh out loud, at how much of my brother I see in my two nephews. I wonder if their sister will ever feel the urge to give them the "broken doll" treatment. In any case, I get to have my plum pudding and eat it too.

# 11

# *Lenten Reflection*

*"For I know the plans I have for you," declares the Lord,*
*"plans to prosper you and not to harm you,*
*plans to give you hope and a future."*
—Jeremiah 29:11

As we celebrate Easter, I humbly ponder the gift of Christian community. Even though we have struggles on every level—as individuals, families, communities, and as a church—we have so much to be grateful for. Celebrating holy days like Easter, I'm always reminded of all our forebears endured for their faith.

During the Reformation in Europe, Conrad Grebel, Georg Blaurock, and Felix Manz spent a lot of time studying the Bible and praying. On January 21, 1525, they baptized each other, and the Anabaptist movement was born. Approximately a year later, the death penalty for these "re-baptizers" was introduced in Europe. That same year, Felix Manz was drowned in the Limmat River in Zurich. Rather than dissuade people from becoming followers, however, the execution of Manz and other Anabaptists inspired many to join these Swiss Brethren. By then, Conrad Grebel had died of the plague.

Georg Blaurock fled to Tirol, Austria, where he continued teaching and baptizing until his execution in 1529. During severe persecution in German-speaking countries, many other Anabaptists fled to Moravia, today part of the Czech Republic. A wealthy landowner, Lord Leonard von Lichtenstein, allowed them to live communally on his land. That didn't last, though; people were uneasy about the presence of so many "heretics" in one area, and they pressured the Liechtensteins to get rid of their Anabaptist tenants. The Liechtensteins opted, however, to ask the Anabaptists to help defend their land should an invasion take place. This divided the Anabaptists. One group agreed to help defend the land. But the others, led by Jacob Wiedemann, were convinced that, as Christians, they should not take up arms. Instead, they left the protection of Lord Lichtenstein and settled just outside of Nikolsburg.

In 1528, the group of two hundred Anabaptists left Nikolsburg to camp in a deserted village. Later they continued north to settle at Austerlitz. They had abandoned or sold most of their possessions. During these desperate times, the appointed stewards spread a cloak on the ground and asked everyone to place on it whatever they had brought with them. Thus began, for this group, a community of goods as described in Acts 2:42-47.

In 1529, Jakob Hutter, a very influential man with exceptional organizational skills, joined this community, and he was elected as elder a few years later. On one of his missionary journeys, Hutter was captured. On February 25, 1536, he was burned at the stake in Innsbruck. But from him we Hutterites take our name.

\* \* \*

The years 1565–1592 proved to be a golden period for Moravian Hutterites. They had good leaders and well-organized schools, and they practiced trades such as pottery, leatherwork, weaving, and wheel- and clock-making. But then years of persecution followed, forcing them to abandon living communally. In 1755, upon the arrival of Lutherans from Carinthia, Austria, the demoralized Hutterites experienced a revival. Their literature inspired the Carinthian Lutherans to adopt Hutterite faith. Together with a remnant of about fifty Hutterites in Transylvania (modern-day Romania), the renewed group managed to establish several communities.

In 1767, however, Maria Theresia, head of the Austro-Hungarian Empire, persecuted the Hutterites. In her mind, they were a disobedient lot; they insisted on living in Christian community of goods and refused to pay war taxes or swear oaths. The authorities made concerted efforts to eradicate Anabaptism in Transylvania. Empress Theresia wanted a Roman Catholic empire, and even the Lutheran church was not acceptable. When torture, imprisonment, and book burning couldn't dissuade the Hutterites from their faith, the empress sent Delphini, a Jesuit priest, to abduct Hutterite children and place them in Catholic orphanages, and to imprison the adults.

Before this dreadful plan could be realized, word reached the Hutterite community. They decided to escape. On a fateful October morning in 1767, they fled south over the Carpathian Mountains to Wallachia, today part of Romania. Here's how our people's history, *The Chronicle of the Hutterian Brethren*, tells it:

> It was a pitiable sight: the Brothers, Sisters, boys and girls each with staff in hand and bundle on back, some with a small child on top of the bundle. . . . So we set out in the name of God, leaving our well-built houses and much of

our household goods behind, unsold. . . . Everything had been prepared in the suburbs of Hermanstadt. Beds stood ready for the children. But God brought Delphini's plans to nothing, for the net he had spread to trap us was torn, and when he came to take us, we were already out of the country.

Less than a year later, war broke out between the Turks and the Russians. The Hutterites were caught between the two armies, with both sides claiming the land on which Hutterite communities were located. In 1770, the Hutterites loaded their belongings onto five wagons drawn by oxen and left Wallachia for Russia. In Russia they established a new community at Vishenka on the Desna River, northeast of Kiev.

Approximately one hundred years later, all Hutterites left Russia for the United States. They settled in Bonne Homme County in South Dakota, with about one-third establishing communities. The others, known as the Prairie People, took advantage of the Homestead Act and settled on individual farms. More than two hundred years later, Hutterite communities still dot the Canadian and Dakotan prairies, plus British Columbia, Washington, Montana, Minnesota, and Oregon.

Hutterites are sometimes asked how we feel toward the Catholic Church today. Naturally we're saddened each time we think about the historic accounts, such as the one mentioned above. As much as these stories are a bleak part of our history, however, they're also a powerful reminder of how our forebears held firm to their convictions and wanted nothing more than to have the freedom to serve God as outlined in the New Testament. We carry no grudge for what happened in the past and endeavor to live peacefully with all human beings.

\* \* \*

On Palm Sunday, upon confession of faith and vowing to remain faithful to God and the church, young people are baptized. Weeks before, those longing to take this important step of faith receive counseling from colony leaders. This includes instruction and discussions on what starting a new life in God means and how this translates into being a faithful, contributing member of the church community.

In the days leading up to baptism, there are special teachings from Romans 6 and Matthew 28. This is followed by further instruction for the baptismal candidates and also a time for reflection and thanksgiving for all baptized brothers and sisters in the Lord.

Right after the pouring of the water for each person baptized in the Hutterian church comes this benediction:

> Since God in His grace has been merciful to you and through the death of Jesus Christ His only begotten Son, and the intercession of the church has forgiven and remitted your sins, may He fill you with the powers from on high and write your name in the book of eternal life. May He keep you as a true brother/sister in the church to serve Jesus until the end. Amen.

This is one of the most powerful benedictions I know. It confirms the words of Peter: "And this water symbolizes baptism that now saves you also—not the removal of dirt from the body but the pledge of a clear conscience toward God" (1 Peter 3:21).

Each time I witness a baptism, my mind goes back in time when I was part of the group kneeling in front of the congregation. Remembering the special prayer, prior to answering the sacred questions and followed by the outward symbol of baptism and that powerful benediction, always prompts tears of gratitude.

Whereas our ancestors suffered persecution, fled from country to country, and at times were compelled to gather secretly in the woods to partake of the Lord's Supper, our lives are enriched by thriving communities and the freedom to celebrate these Lenten holy days peacefully.

# 12

# A Peaches and Cream Mother's Day

*Behind all your stories is always your mother's story.*
*Because hers is where yours begin.*
—Mitch Albom, author, *Tuesdays with Morrie*

IT WAS A LOVELY MOTHER'S DAY, with the sun pouring down her golden blessings. Light streamed through the windows of the communal kitchen where the people were gathered. As is customary on a Hutterite colony, we were anticipating a beautifully prepared Sunday dinner: noodle soup, roast duck stuffed with sauerkraut, steamed carrots, salad, potatoes, and fruit pizza for dessert.

Most adults were already seated. The children, who had eaten earlier, were in the *Essenschuel*, children's dining room, waiting for their cue to enter to sing special Mother's Day songs. Some women, including my mother, were still at the buffet table in the kitchen area, filling their plates. On kitchen duty that week, I was in the kitchen cleaning a mountain of dishes and moving them to their place on the shelf.

"Is there salad dressing in the fridge?" Mom asked.

"Probably," I answered, without looking up.

She entered the walk-in refrigerator to look for the salad dressing. Not finding it on the bottom shelves where it usually sat, she spotted a gallon-sized salad dressing container on the top shelf. *That must be it,* she thought.

But on a Hutterite colony, reusing containers is as normal as eating bread. Unfortunately for my mother, this particular salad dressing container was being reused to hold cream, and its lid had been screwed on haphazardly.

Reaching up and pulling it toward herself, she received a cool, creamy baptism. Nobody witnessed it. For a few minutes she stood rooted to the spot, trying to decide how to deal with this mess. But with no water or dishrags in sight, she knew there was just one option left. *I wonder if I could slip out without being detected.*

Meanwhile, I was still busy at the sink. My mind meandered back to another Mother's Day—one I didn't enjoy so much. I was cooking that time as well. The evening before, my sister Sonia and I had baked a cherry cake for each mom on the colony. We wanted these to be special cakes. While my sister got the cake pans ready, I measured out the ingredients and mixed them together. We knew the mothers were excited about the special cakes they would receive.

Something didn't seem quite right with the batter; it was rather thick. But we filled the pans anyway and were not too bothered. Plus, there wasn't anything that could be done at that point. After watching the cakes in the oven, though, we knew something was seriously wrong. The cakes didn't rise properly, and it took longer than usual to bake them. As I lifted the pans out of the oven, my heart was as heavy as the cake. Visions of presenting the colony moms with a special gift flew out the window. There was nothing fluffy and light about these cakes. They were stiff and heavy, like water-logged floral sponges.

I spent an extremely long night of tossing and turning and beating myself up, as I was the one who mixed it. I must have done something wrong when I measured the flour, or maybe the baking powder. Too many eggs? Endless possible mistakes swirled around inside my head, like the batter in the bakery's mixer. No amount of trying to figure out what went wrong changed the fact that on Mother's Day, of all the days in the year, these dear ladies would get brick cake. Mercifully the night ended, but with the dawn came the realization that I'd have to face a bunch of moms who had been anticipating perfectly baked cherry cake.

The mood at lunch was stilted, full of unnervingly polite or sympathetic smiles, which did nothing for the disappointment and regret knotted in my stomach. "It doesn't taste so bad, Linda," one sweet mom offered generously. "Just a bit heavy." *Right, I'm pretty sure not even the birds would eat it*, I thought glumly. I just wanted this day to end and forget that I even tried to make it cherry-cake special.

A movement at the walk-in refrigerator pulled me from these unpleasant memories. Very cautiously, Mom opened the door and peeked out to see who was still in the kitchen, hoping that most had gone to the dining room. Grateful that there were only a few women, she ventured out, peering over the top of her cream-splashed glasses.

She was met with peals of laughter from a few women still in the kitchen getting their food. In the dining room, meanwhile, everyone was quietly waiting for grace to be said. Questioning eyes moved toward the kitchen doorway, which was closed. Everyone wanted to know what the joke was.

Hurrying toward the sink—cream cascading down her face, dripping from her black and white kerchief, and streaming down the front of her black church jacket—my mother resembled a mischievous cat. Struggling to keep from laughing, I managed to wipe most of it off for her, knowing this image would stay with me for many years. The crowning touch came when I heard, "Peaches and cream!" from a chuckling elderly lady, who added, "Happy Mother's Day!"

As for the special cherry cakes? The sting of that Mother's Day episode of disappointment lingered for a while, but in its wake I came away a bit wiser. I was reminded that there would likely be more culinary calamities in my future. I chalked it up as a character-building moment; disappointments help us learn and grow. As Mom would say, *"Durch Schodn weat mir klueg, ober nit reich"* (Adversity makes us wise but not rich).

# PART III

## *Values*

# 13

# Weathered Wood Lessons

*Use it up, wear it out, make it do, or do without.*

—New England proverb

**D**on't throw that detergent bottle out,"
Mom admonished, reaching for a sharp knife. She cut the
bottom part off diagonally, turning it into a fine shovel for
the sandbox.

Mom served as *Klanaschuel Ankela* (nursery school teacher),
for many years, and among the sandbox toys there were always
some repurposed items like the detergent-bottle shovel. Cutting
a pop bottle in half made a fine funnel, and the bottom part was
an ideal mold for beautiful mud cakes.

I've always been taught the value of frugality. I learned it
not so much through words as through observation. Frugality
surrounded me as constantly as did saying grace before meals
and eating in the communal dining room. My parents taught
by example, thus showing us that thrift was as much a biblical principle as "Love your neighbor as yourself" (Mark 12:31).
Mom never threw out empty containers or anything she
thought might be reused. A plastic bleach jug, for example,
would become a clothespin holder. After she cut a hole in its

side and a slit at the bottom of the handle to serve as a hook, this receptacle slid along the wash line with ease.

Just inside the door of our home there's always a crocheted rug crafted from the wool of unravelled sweaters. Part of the washroom décor is a set of beautiful and practical rag rugs, created out of old Fortrel clothes. Fortrel is a durable, non-fraying, non-fading, polyester fabric used years ago for dresses, slacks, and pant suits. With patchwork hot pads and dishcloths knit from recycled yarn, the kitchen boasts old-country appeal. In the past, when sugar and flour came in cotton sacks, these were bleached and turned into dishtowels, with colorfully embroidered designs added on one side or in the corners.

Although some of these recycled items were eventually retired along with the old-fashioned syrup-pail knitting "baskets," the values they instilled are as durable as colony clothes. "It's not garbage when it can still be used," rings in my ear whenever I want to throw out something that could be reused. That was Mom's way of reminding us of the teaching in Psalm 24: "The earth is the LORD's, and the fullness thereof; the world, and they that dwell therein" (Psalm 24:1 KJV). This implies a sacred duty to take care of the earth and encourage others to do the same, especially the younger generation.

To ensure our students are aware of the importance of recycling and reusing, we incorporate special programs into our school schedules. For a few years, an organization called Take Pride Winnipeg has offered its Bag Up Manitoba program to schools. During the month of October, each school that registers has their students collect plastic bags, wrappers, or bubble wrap from their homes. At school, the items are counted and packaged into bigger bags. The bags are eventually shipped to an American company that builds decks, park benches, planters, and birdhouses out of recycled plastic. This contest helps prevent plastic bags from going to landfill sites, or worse: to the Great Pacific Garbage Patch.

For the first few years of the Bag Up Manitoba program, each participating school received fifty Frisbees and the book *Timmy the Tumbling Bag* by Tom Ethans, executive director of Take Pride Winnipeg. The fourteen schools that collected the most bags won a park bench made of recycled bags. Since the program has grown so much over the years, the organizers now have draws to determine who will get the benches. This way all schools, no matter how many students they have, have a better chance at winning.

The first year we took part, we knew when we registered that the last winning school had collected ten thousand bags. Because we were a small school, with only twenty-seven students, I predicted we'd collect about three thousand. However, the children, their families, and their friends responded to the idea with gusto. Each October morning brought the familiar chant, "I have more bags!" Every few days the students in grades four through eight helped count bags, excited to see how our total increased. We posted the total on the whiteboards at school and in the communal kitchen, motivating everybody to continue bringing bags.

This was not only a fun project for the children; it also created increased awareness among the adults about recycling and keeping our community clean. "I look at plastic bags differently now," one grandmother commented. "I no longer just throw them into the garbage."

That first year, near the end of October, everybody kept asking, "Did we win the bench?" When our bags were scheduled to be picked up a week after the deadline, we still didn't know whether we had won. Our total was 9,719. Our students were convinced we didn't win.

"Still, we *are* sending lots of bags to be recycled," I reminded them. "And we will receive Frisbees and a book." Nevertheless, I wondered why we hadn't heard anything yet.

When the people from Take Pride Winnipeg arrived to thank the children for taking part in the program, we all gathered in one classroom. "I brought you fifty Frisbees and my book," Tom Ethans announced. This garnered polite applause. We talked about the numbers; how many bags we collected compared to the top school, which had managed to collect nineteen thousand bags.

"But being the nice people we are," Ethans continued, "We'll give you a bench, too. It's in my van." Enthusiastic cheers, applause, and smiles ensued! We had placed first in the category of rural schools with enrollments of under one hundred.

Now each October our school comes down with bag fever. We've won three benches, some birdhouses, and planters, all made from recycled bags. The project has become an important way we teach children about recycling and keeping our community clean. All children, right down to the youngest ones, can take part in this program and learn about taking care of the environment.

\*   \*   \*

My fondest recycling memory involves pieces of weathered wood. After raising geese for more than thirty-two years, our

The oak desk my uncle made for my dad, using the scrap lumber of the old loading scaffold.

colony decided to discontinue this enterprise. My dad was given the task of disassembling fences, along with the wooden scaffolds used for loading geese for shipping. "I'm going to ask Uncle Joe to build a desk with the old planks from the loading scaffold," he announced at snack time one day.

"You can't be serious!" I exclaimed, thinking this was as far-fetched as a goose laying a golden egg. "Those planks have been out there in the elements, trampled on in rain, fog, and snow for decades! Not to mention that they've been pecked at and probably pooped on by geese."

"They are solid oak and thick enough to be planed down," Dad continued calmly. "It would sure be a shame to just burn them!" When Dad pitched the dream desk idea to Uncle Joe, he responded with as much gusto as if Dad had just suggested he take up embroidering. Nevertheless, not known to waste words, he reluctantly agreed.

For years, Dad's antique-brown desk beautified our home and served as his work space. It also gave him many opportunities to tell visitors its story. Sadly, Dad hasn't sat by his desk for years now, and all we're left with is a desk-full of memories. Today, it stands in my classroom, a sturdy worktable and a daily reminder of all Dad taught us.

Hutterites have been practicing frugality for centuries. Learning new ways to utilize old things is imperative in today's world. However, with materials more readily available nowadays, people tend to needlessly throw out and replace things, rather than reusing or recycling them. As stewards of the earth, we're obligated to teach today's affluent generation our own weathered wood lessons.

# 14

# Hearts and Hands for Common Causes

*Each of you should give what you have decided in
your heart to give, not reluctantly or under compulsion,
for God loves a cheerful giver.*

—2 Corinthians 9:7

FOR SEVERAL YEARS, the women on our colony have sewed therapeutic lap quilts for the Alzheimer Society of Manitoba. After sewing for more than two months one winter, we were extremely gratified to see a stack of 250 simple, yet beautifully pieced lap quilts, which the society distributed to local senior citizen homes. One of the letters we received read: "Thank you for participating in this project. You have enhanced the quality of life and brought smiles to the faces of those who received these lovely quilts."

Hutterites are involved in many local charity projects. Some, such as the "lap quilt project," are ongoing and involve many colonies all over Manitoba during the winter months. Other projects, like the Hospice & Palliative Care Manitoba (HPCM) craft sale, happen less frequently but still garner heartwarming

A lap quilt made by the women of the Elm River Colony.

participation from the Hutterite community.

The quilt project is ideal for Hutterites for a number of reasons. Hutterite women are avid sewers; consequently, there are lots of leftover pieces around that people say are "just too good to throw out." What better way to use them than in quilts? Furthermore, in the middle of winter there's more time for indoor activities like sewing. There's just something warm and cozy about a few women getting together to create quilts while the wind howls a subzero song outside. Most importantly, though, the project will benefit residents of senior homes for years to come. The quilts are about ninety centimeters (thirty-five inches) square, fitting comfortably on the lap of someone in a wheelchair.

"Each quilt should have an assortment of fabrics, such as corduroy, flannel, terrycloth, satin, cotton—the more textures, the better," said our instructor and fellow Hutterite, Anna, who had learned about the project at a conference in Winnipeg.

The first year, about twenty seamstresses created lap quilts in their homes and some also contributed fabric. "I'm so happy that I've finally found a way to use those little pieces that keep piling up," one mother proclaimed. "Of course, I *can't* just throw them out!"

Once the sewing was underway, I, too, took time after school to help sew squares together. Later I also worked on quilting the patchwork tops together with fleece or flannel bottoms. Each time I held up a finished lap quilt, I wondered whose life it would touch and whose frail hands would be warmer because of the soft fabric.

This is a project in which all ages can be involved. One little girl diligently stacked and sorted the pieces. "I have a dress like this!" she informed my sister Shirley, an avid quilter, who was sewing nearby. "And this one is like the quilt on my bed."

"When you're done, bring the quilts to the living room and I will sew on the buttons," my mom offered. She wouldn't allow the "grandmother" label to slow her down or stop her from offering her own well-practiced touch. My sister Joanne helped her with that task.

Since then, every winter finds many Hutterites in various colonies helping the Alzheimer Society of Manitoba with this lap quilt project. These quilts are found to be therapeutic for elderly people, especially those suffering from Alzheimer's. They are created out of a variety of distinct textures and colors, which can have a calming effect, in addition to providing warmth and comfort to the seniors.

*   *   *

One spring some years ago, my sister Lorena received a call from Dora, a family friend at another colony. "I hope you're wearing your good Samaritan hat today, because I have a job for you!"

Andrea Firth, conference coordinator with Hospice & Palliative Care Manitoba, had asked whether the Hutterian community might donate some crafts for their annual conference. Organizers were anticipating hundreds of delegates from across Canada, and since they depend on donations, they wanted a substantial selection of items for people to buy.

After Lorena informed us of this project, our whole family supported it by donating homemade crafts. Through information Andrea sent, we learned that HPCM is a volunteer-based charitable organization that provides telephone bereavement support to anyone in Manitoba. Initial calls are taken by program coordinators, who match a trained bereavement volunteer with each client. Contact is maintained for about eighteen months, depending on client needs. Training and education are provided for volunteers, families, and professionals working in palliative care.

My family and I were confident Hutterites would enjoy participating in such a worthy cause, given their creativity and generosity. As it turned out, we were right! "If someone is willing to make a quilt," one mother announced, "I have feathers left from making my children a duvet."

"I could sew it, but I'll need someone to mark the squares," a grandma responded. "My knees won't allow me to crawl around on the floor anymore!" Through this kind of collaboration, we completed a beautiful down duvet and pillow set, along with a vibrant floral cover and pillow shams.

Lorena sent a letter to other colonies, outlining the project and asking for donations. Soon boxes of crafts started arriving. Hutterites from thirteen colonies donated a wide variety of items such as hand-knit slippers, mittens, and socks; large crocheted rugs; and elegant doilies. There were sewn items: frilly aprons, soft cushions, and adorable baby clothes that were both practical and pretty. There was even art, including Intarsia, in which pictures of animals or flowers are created with pieces of wood sanded and glued together and covered with a smooth lacquer finish.

I staff a craft table at a fundraiser for Hospice & Palliative Care Manitoba.

In early July, Andrea Firth and a colleague drove to my colony to pick up the donations. "It was like Christmas when we first opened those boxes of beautiful crafts," Andrea told us later. "We are most appreciative of the donations from the colonies and have received many positive comments on the quantity, variety, and quality of the work!"

During the three-day conference, the organizers set up an Artisans' Market in one corner of a huge conference room. Shirley, Lorena, and I volunteered to help sell the crafts, most of which were donations from Manitoba Hutterites. "The Hutterite crafts are the highlight of the conference!" exclaimed one of the volunteers stopping by our table. "We are so grateful for your kindness and generosity."

Running the booth for one day was new for us, but it felt good to help an organization that provides such essential services to Manitobans. It was exciting to meet and chat with delegates from every Canadian province.

"My daughter is expecting a baby very soon, and I'd like a gift for her," announced one man; "Problem is, I don't know if I'm buying for a girl or a boy." I showed him some layettes, but he waffled between two blankets. Finally, he bought both. "The smaller one for right now and the bigger one for later," he beamed. "Perfect!"

Hutterite contributions raised more than two thousand dollars, Andrea told us after the conference, and the committee still had items on hand for sale at a later date.

This would not have been possible, nor would it have been so special, had there not been so many good Samaritans who put their hearts and hands together for a common cause. It's always a wonderful feeling to love our neighbors via various outreach programs. Hutterites have also long been involved with other charitable endeavors, including inner city services to the poor in Winnipeg, Mennonite Central Committee's relief and development work, and mission projects in Haiti, Romania, Nigeria, and Liberia. We're abundantly blessed, and we are convinced that these blessings are meant to be shared with others in need.

# 15

# *Bracing for the Breach*

*The deed is everything, the glory naught.*
—Johann Wolfgang von Goethe, German writer

IN 2011, our provincial government had to make a choice. It could wait out a flood in our area of the Prairies and see what happened, or it could impose a controlled breach of the "Hoop 'n' Holler" bend of the Assiniboine River, along Highway 331 near Portage la Prairie. The latter option would take pressure off the weakening Assiniboine River dikes. They decided to do the controlled breach. This disturbing news meant that some farmers' fields would be flooded. The method to the "controlled breach" madness was to save a more populated area from potential flooding. This meant the people southeast of this bend would be sacrificing their homes and livelihoods for others.

Naturally, their decision raised mixed feelings. "Why do we have to be the scapegoats?" one area resident protested. Another wondered, "How can they decide to sacrifice my land to spare others' properties?" Others saw beyond that: "I totally understand why they chose this spot. It's an oxbow of the Assiniboine, so the current isn't as strong."

Neighbors working together to build a sandbag dike.

To brace for the anticipated breach, people from all walks of life generously donated time, energy, and resources to protect homes from the floodwaters. Everyone involved—and not just area residents and those whose properties were threatened—was treated to a dramatic demonstration of neighborly love. High schoolers worked shoulder to shoulder with retirees, city and town folk labored beside farmers, and Hutterites served food to army regiments brought in to help.

Sandbagging sites crawled with volunteers who produced sandbags in record time. These were trucked to homes where human chains formed to place the white bags and build dikes around vulnerable houses. Military personnel erected "aqua dikes," huge black tubes filled with water to protect homes. And Hutterites from colonies all over Manitoba came to help. This massive effort continued until every house in danger of flooding had a white or black barrier standing guard. Thus,

An aqua dike to stave off potential flooding.

my community happened to have front row seats to a once-in-a-lifetime drama: Bracing for the Breach, starring Raging Assiniboine. Scratch the popcorn; we were pitching sandbags!

Most flooding in Manitoba typically occurs along the Red River, an hour to the east. That year, however, the Assiniboine was flooding. My colony is just five miles east of the Hoop 'n' Holler, the little bend that was put on the map that spring. To set the scene, imagine this: we had the raging Assiniboine two miles north of us, the Elm River two miles south, while the La Salle quietly rippled through our colony.

There's a Canadian National railroad track between us and the Elm River, the area most affected when Highway 331 was breached. I've heard the train rumbling past thousands of times, never looking at it as more than another aspect of our prairie landscape. During the flood, I had another perspective; it was the blessed barrier that might keep the water from reaching our colony. I never even stopped to think, however, that the culverts under the railway could not be plugged, as that could harm the tracks. Along with everybody else, we watched, hoped, and prayed, especially for the people who would be directly affected by this spill.

We had no idea what the La Salle River would do. And nobody seemed to think that our colony itself would be in any danger, since we were at a higher elevation. Many of our people were out helping neighbors protect their homes. "It feels different than fighting the flood in 1997," my sister commented after sandbagging for neighbors. "We know these people!" Our kitchen ladies prepared food and delivered it to people at various sandbagging sites.

"Well, I know now where the saying 'enough food for an army' comes from," someone else quipped, after serving army personnel for a few hours; "We ran a bit short." A few days later we served stew, fresh buns, cookies, and coffee to the hungry troops, and that time there was enough. "You have no idea how much we appreciate your home-cooked meals!" one man told us. "Beats army rations."

Before the breach occurred, we thought 90 percent of our fields would be affected. This would have had dire ramifications on that year's crops. "We should be seeding already," one of our men stated days before the breach, his voice gruff with concern. "Each day we're unable to seed diminishes potential yields." Fortunately, however, the water that flowed through the breach did not cause any major damage and only reached the dikes of a few houses, in the Hoop 'n' Holler area. The flooded fields, including one of ours, could not be seeded until very late. It all worked out fine, though, as the crops in the fields that had been flooded turned out well.

Despite the fact that we had been in a crisis, humor helped people cope. "Free water! Take a much as you like," read a home-made sign on a post near one of the homes with a dike around it. "River Front Property—Any Offers?" another boasted. At a citizenship ceremony on Manitoba Day, member of Parliament Candace Hoeppner generated some chuckles when she mentioned the flood in her speech. "To some, Manitoba is not that old. Today marks 141 years and right now we're experiencing water retention, a sure sign of old age."

Eventually, river levels receded, the breach was closed, and homeowners could breathe easier. The white and black barriers were but eyesores, mute reminders of the backbreaking cleanup to come. Thankfully, the community spirit prevailed for this daunting task of taking the dikes down, even though some joked about keeping a low profile after the flood. "I guess we're all changing our cell phone numbers when we're done here," someone bantered while building dikes and already thinking about taking them down. "That way people can't call us to carry these bags away."

# 16

# Hospitality in a Time of War

*They were the best years of my life. I got more food than I did
back home, and working in the bush was like a dream.*
—Richard Beranek, German POW, recalling his time in Manitoba

IN THE SUMMER OF 1946, when my dad was just eleven
years old, two of his friends were walking along the railroad
tracks south of their colony when they met some German prisoners of war. They were stationed at a camp and were helping
area farmers with the harvest. Sometimes they were allowed to
leave their camps on day passes.

"Where do you live?" one of prisoners asked in English.

"*Mir kennen kolla Deitsch*" (We only know German), one of
the boys replied.

"*Ach, wie das Herz blutet! Deutsches Volk!*" (O, my bleeding
heart! German people!), the prisoner responded.

The prisoners asked where the colony was and upon returning to their camp lost no time telling their comrades this good
news. Their camp was located roughly one mile east of the colony, with fields and the La Salle River in between. Soon the
prisoners built a tree-bridge across the narrow river so they

could walk across the fields and become acquainted with the German-speaking Hutterites. Being able to converse in their own language is what drew the prisoners to the colony. But over the course of the summer, both parties learned that they had even more in common: a strong work ethic, a love of singing, and traditional food.

During World War II, approximately 33,000 German prisoners of war were detained in twenty-five camps across Canada—two of the biggest were in Medicine Hat and Lethbridge, Alberta. Not all German soldiers supported the Nazi regime, and those who clearly were Nazis were kept behind barbed wire for the duration of their stay in Canada. The others were allowed to leave their confinement. According to the Geneva Convention, POWs could not be forced to work. When asked if they would *like* to work, however, many decided it would be better than being bored behind barbed wire. They worked in parks, lumber camps, and on farm labor projects. They were paid fifty cents a day, which did not go directly to them but was put into an account in their name.

Growing up, I heard my father speak of "the prisoners" many times. "They helped build and paint Grandpa's red chicken barn," he told us. Back then, however, I didn't give those stories too much thought. I didn't realize that this was a truly unique experience: pacifist Hutterites and prisoners of war working, singing, and sharing meals together.

"We learned many German words from them including *Bremse* (brake) and *Zündkerze* (spark plug)," Dad always said. Since he helped his dad in the chicken barn, he was able to spend lots of time with the men. Even though we speak a German dialect, many of our words are English. When buying things like tractor parts and machinery, for example, Hutterites bring English words home along with them, and these words become part of our vocabulary. This practice is ongoing, not just something that happened in earlier generations.

"We could talk Hutterisch with some of them," one elderly man recalled. "But we had a hard time talking with others, for their dialect was so different." Because Austria, where the Hutterites' dialect originates from, is south of Germany, some of its dialects are distinctly similar to the dialects spoken in southern Germany. Other German dialects, such as those from northern Germany, are drastically different from Hutterisch.

When the prisoners came to work on our colony, an army truck brought them along with four armed guards. One day when it was nearing suppertime, some of the POWs who had been helping to build a barn wanted to stay to finish a task. When they asked their guard, however, he told them brusquely, "No. When you hear the truck's horn, you better come." But the no-nonsense army voice did not deter the Germans from devising their own plan. As soon as the horn blew, they rushed to the truck and clambered into the back in a way that made it difficult for the guards to count them. Their plan worked. Four had stayed behind to help finish the task and returned to camp later.

In time though, the guards became more lenient and the prisoners were allowed to leave the camp unsupervised. They did have a curfew, and the guards told the Hutterites, "If they cause any trouble at all, let us know and that will be the end of the visits."

"For a while they came for church services," one Hutterite man remembered. "But then they stopped." When the POWs were asked why, one of the Germans hung his head and said,

"We can't. It bothers us too much, because we've killed so many people."

The Hutterites challenged the prisoners: "And how can you just outright go and kill another human being anyway?"

"Your Canadian soldiers do the same thing," they responded. "That's war!"

\* \* \*

The concept of living in Christian community was something the German POWs could never fully comprehend, even after spending so much time among the Hutterites. Still, that did not stop them from appreciating some things that happened on the colony.

After a hard day's work, it was not uncommon for Maendel *Olvetter*, my great-grandfather, to serve a glass of homemade wine before supper. This delighted these German men. One day, close to suppertime, one of the prisoners looked around asking, "*Wo ist der Kellermeister*?" (Where is the master of the cellar?) He wondered if he'd be getting a sip of wine that day. Because Grandpa Maendel made wine for the community, the prisoners dubbed him "master of the cellar." He and his family lived in an old farmhouse with a cellar, which was an ideal place for making wine. This cellar was unique, because its entry was on the outside of the house, with no way to get to it from inside.

"One Sunday we had them over for a communal meal," someone else recalled. "I remember how much they enjoyed the noodle soup, roast duck, and sauerkraut." It's understandable that such a meal would have meant a lot to these homesick men. After being in this strange land for some years, they now shared a traditional German meal and conversed in their mother tongue with people who not only welcomed them into the workforce but also spent many evenings visiting and singing together.

A few people told me that the community learned one of our evening songs from the prisoners. "*Gute Nacht, gute Nacht, wieder ist ein Tag vollbracht*" (Good night, good night, another day has come to the end) is still widely sung today and has become a favorite for many Hutterites. Mostly, however, the POWs sang German folk songs. One melancholy song, written by Hubert Dorfmüller, wowed a Hutterite audience on a summer evening as prisoners of war sat on the cool grass, singing their hearts out while longing for their homeland. Tears trickled down their cheeks as they sang:

> *In meiner Heimat, da blühen die Rosen* (In my homeland the roses are blooming).

> *In meiner Heimat ist es wunderschön* (My homeland is beautiful).

This was one of many such evenings where they entertained colony members with their music: singing and playing guitar, accordion, and harmonica. At a time when musical instruments were frowned upon on the colony, this must have sounded like a Beethoven symphony. "I cannot begin to tell you how beautiful it was," one woman recalls. "I had never heard any lovelier music and singing."

Everyone with whom I spoke expressed similar sentiments. "One time my dad asked me to bring a load of wood with a pair of horses and a wagon," one grandpa recalled. "I heard music and decided to check it out, as that was quite unusual." He followed the sound to the chicken barn, where the prisoners were giving an evening concert. Forgetting all about his chore, this lad stayed and enjoyed the lovely music, along with many other colony members. Not until midnight, when his dad woke him and asked about the wood, did he remember. His dad kindly went to the woodpile and found the horses still patiently waiting for their driver.

After all those years, some people still remembered a few of the prisoner's names. Two were Ernst Werdermann and Fritz Wanderberg, who later settled in Manitoba. Others were Kurt, Paul, Hans, Werner, and Bruno, Rudolf, Bubi, Franz, Rudi, and Heinrich. Apparently there were several Hanses, so people renamed them in a uniquely Hutterite fashion: The Hans who worked for Jim Gibson became Jim-Hans. The Hans who loved fresh warm milk and always found his way to the cow barn around milking time was christened Kuhstoll-Hans (Cow Barn Hans). Another one was known as Honsela, which translates to "Little Hans." Honsela's name reveals how fond the Hutterites were of these men; in addition to indication "small," the addition of *la* to a name is also a Hutterisch term of endearment. From all accounts, this fact was not lost on Honsela and his comrades.

"Oh, you have no idea how they charmed the girls," one man chuckled. "And some girls really enjoyed being in the company of these friendly Germans. Nobody seemed too concerned about the men mingling with our people, and I never heard anybody say anything against them. They were always very respectful when they visited."

Some remembered that the Hutterites were sympathetic to the men's plight as prisoners. They may have recalled their own

Hutterite history and how their forebears were imprisoned in Europe centuries earlier, albeit for an entirely different reason.

Even though the Hutterites befriended these German soldiers, there was never any doubt about where each stood on the issue of war. While they stood on opposite ends of this spectrum, they made a clear statement of how, in the name of peace, differences can be put aside and friendships built.

The POWs must have liked what they saw here in Canada, because some would have gladly stayed here after the war, but they all had to be repatriated. However, they had the option to return to Canada later, and many did. I heard a number of stories of former prisoners who had settled in Canada, greeting people from our colony during chance encounters in Winnipeg many years later.

Rebecca Maendel remembered her dad taking the prisoners to the colony sugar beet field. Her brother Peter, who was a boy at the time, went along for the ride. Years later, while in Winnipeg on business Peter was warmly greeted by a man. Somewhat taken aback, Peter responded, "I don't know you."

"But I remember you!" the man answered. "I was one of those prisoners your dad drove to the sugar beet field. You were the little boy who always rode along."

As the summer of 1946 ended and the prisoners said a final *Auf Wiedersehen*, the Hutterites knew they would miss their open-air German evening concerts and the extra hands to help with the work. However, they were happy that their German friends would now be able to return to their homeland to help rebuild their devastated country and once again relish the splendor of peacetime and the beauty of blooming roses.

# 17

# *God Keep Our Land Glorious and Free*

*God-fearing Christians, look up!*
*Take fresh courage in the fight!*
*Pursue Him through suffering, the cross, and shame,*
*loving God and your neighbor,*
*for that is the way to the Kingdom of Heaven.*

—Hans Mändl, Hutterite martyr, *Chronicle of the Hutterian Brethren*

CANADA, WITH ITS MANY IMMIGRANTS, is like a beautiful patchwork quilt. People from other countries have settled on our rich farmlands or in thriving towns and cities and now proudly call this country home. A kaleidoscope of sights, sounds, tastes, and customs gives our country a rich folkloric vista. Each ethnic group is like a quilt piece, adding its unique color or texture. Each is stitched together with common respect, creating a spectacular whole.

I got a glimpse of this one day at a "Sharing Our World" event in Portage la Prairie, about sixteen kilometers (ten miles) from our colony. Twenty-three ethnic groups from the surrounding area gathered to share their world. Each had a booth with a display of artifacts, clothes, art, pictures, books, crafts, and musical instruments. Some came in their traditional dress, lending a vibrant and festive air to the day.

I was grateful for the opportunity to share our Hutterite way of life with people stopping by our booth. "It's just great that you're here!" someone told me. "It's important for people to understand your unique culture. I have a new appreciation for Hutterites!"

During the day there was an opportunity for people to take the stage and showcase their cultural dress and explain what their clothing signified and where it originated. We showcased a Hutterite wedding dress and an Austrian *Dirndl*, after which our dress style is modeled.

Walking among the booths, I heard conversations in various languages including those of the Ukraine, First Nations, Pakistan, Germany, Mexico, Nigeria, and the Philippines. English united us all. Perhaps it was not as miraculous as Pentecost, when everybody heard their own tongue as the apostles spoke. Nevertheless, mingling and sharing with different cultures creates a sense of "peace on earth," at least in our little corner.

"It is wonderful to showcase the different cultures and learn about the traditions, customs, and values they all bring to our community," exclaimed Mary Lynn Moffat, coordinator of the event. "We see many of these people from time to time, and here we get to know them a little better."

We had the rare opportunity to feast on a variety of delicious dishes while watching a variety of performances by choirs—including our own high schoolers singing two songs. Other groups did duets, jigs, and a powwow. As I sat down with a mountain of ethnic foods on my plate, my taste buds did a celebratory jig of their own. There were perogies from the Ukraine, biryani from Pakistan, arroz con pollo from Panama, spiced lamb, rice, pork, bannock, tacos, Jamaican sweet potato pudding, and lots more. Our Hutterite contribution was *Zucker Honkelich* (creamy sugar pie), *Schuttn Honkelich* (cottage cheese pie), and fresh buns with strawberry jam.

"Sharing Our World" caused me to reflect on how the Hutterites fit into this cultural collage. With our rich history, unique language, and community-of-goods lifestyle, we're a distinctive addition and are contributing to the whole.

Canada is not without its stains, however, which makes days like "Sharing Our World" even more significant. Some years ago I saw the trailer for the then newly released film *We Were Children*, which tells the tragic, bloodcurdling account of Canada's residential schools. A catastrophic decision by the Canadian government and church leaders forcibly separated Aboriginal Canadian children from families and effectively destroyed a people's future.

The residential schools were established in 1884, and attendance was made compulsory in 1920. The network of boarding schools was designed for the three major Aboriginal groups: First Nations, Métis, and Inuit. Funded by the Canadian government, the schools were managed by churches: Catholic, Anglican, United Church of Canada, and several smaller denominations of Canada. About 30 percent of Aboriginal children were forcibly removed from their homes, family influence, and culture. Besides having to endure living away from familiar surroundings and being deprived of their ancestral language, many of these children suffered abuse at these schools. In 1907, one report suggested that up to 40 percent of children in these schools died from diseases, most often from tuberculosis. The last residential school was closed in 1986.

I was struck once again by how traumatic it must have been for the Aboriginal parents whose children were removed from their homes. The government's purpose was clearly to assimilate them into the dominant Canadian culture, convert them to Christianity, and "civilize" them.

After seeing this trailer, my mind wandered to Europe and some dismal chapters of my own Hutterite history. What if eighteenth-century imperial powers had succeeded in taking our children? What if the Jesuit priest's plan to abduct Hutterite children and imprison adults (see chapter 11) had actually worked? How would our story have changed?

At the end of the "Sharing Our World" day, a group of Aboriginal Canadians started a friendship dance and invited people to join them. As they made their way through the audience, more and more joined the line, holding hands with the person beside them and doing a little step dance, with drummers helping them keep time. What an appropriate way to end the event, because that is what the day was all about. No matter what cultures we all belong to, or what sore spots our history holds, today we can all be friends, respect each other's differences, and celebrate the fact that we're all humans created by a loving God.

# 18

# Steel Bar Blues . . .
# and Blessings

*I needed clothes and you clothed me, I was sick and you looked after me, I was in prison and you came to visit me.*

—Matthew 25:36

FEW PEOPLE KNOW that I spent time behind bars some years ago. And not in my home country, but in the United States of America, "land of the free, home of the brave." I should tell you, though: I never did anything wrong! Or I guess I should say *we* didn't, as there were two of us.

I was on an extended visit at the New Meadow Run Bruderhof in Pennsylvania, a Christian community similar to the Hutterites. One afternoon my friend and I were on our way to a local town. It was raining the whole time, and the rain matched my mood; I was a bit apprehensive about the excursion, as this was a completely new venture. I was willing to give it a whirl, but I knew I was not from the "home of the brave."

Shortly after we reached town, we found ourselves in front of a jail. It had iron gates, guards, and steel bars. We were ushered in by one of the guards. After a few doors and gates slammed shut behind us, it became clear why they call it "the slammer." I looked behind me each time, and a stark realization settled on me like a heavy, dark cloak. This dreadful clanging was doing exactly what it was meant to do: intimidate. Finally we were locked in a cell with four other women. They smiled a shy welcome, but it didn't do much for my mood.

Everything about this place was cold and stark and bleak. The only furniture was a metal picnic table bolted to the floor. There was a small television just outside the cell, barely reachable should one of the women desire to switch the channel. Behind a wall stood a lonely row of low cots with thin sheets and tired pillows. An inmate was sleeping in one of them. "She's sick," one of the others informed us. *No wonder*, I thought. *I think I'll be sick myself real soon.* I noticed the washroom area, which offered little to no privacy. One of the women was pacing nervously, adding to my discomfort. We soon learned that she was being released that day. I didn't understand why she wasn't doing cartwheels or some little dance—anything but this irritating, silent pace. I couldn't figure out why she was so nervous about being released.

I imagine you're wondering what brought us here. The people of Meadow Run did weekly prison visits, and that week, my friend asked if I wanted to go with her. To be honest, I wasn't terribly excited about it. But because I'd never done anything like that before, I agreed. More importantly, I was touched by this outreach program and wanted to be a part of it, if only for this one day. It did feel eerie, stark, and cold, but knowing we brightened the day for these four women was well worth my discomfort.

"We can't bring scissors or anything that could be used to hurt someone," my friend explained as we prepared for this visit. This made things somewhat challenging, as we had planned to do a plastic canvas craft. The materials we did bring worked well, though. When we were done, each woman had a small plastic canvas art piece that they had created. Before we left, my friend read a story, and I was struck how much they enjoyed this simple activity. Except for the one who was sick, they were all quite friendly. One of them told us she had a little girl at home. Even the woman who was pacing nervously smiled a few times.

Since that visit, I've often wondered why our own communities don't adhere to this biblical command to visit prisoners. I've not received any definitive answers. Perhaps some Hutterite communities are involved in such outreach efforts and I've just never heard about it.

Did we make a huge impact in the lives of these inmates? Maybe not. But I do know that on that one day we did make a difference, however small. Radiating from their faces was gratitude that someone cared enough to come spend time with them. I came away feeling blessed that I got this opportunity.

# PART IV

*Heritage*

# 19

# The Amana-Hutterite Connection

*Life presents many choices,*
*the choices we make determine our future.*
—Catherine Pulsifier, Canadian author

YOUNG HUTTERITE MICHAEL HOFER found himself on a train traveling across the Midwest of the United States. It was the early 1880s, and he was leaving his community. He was traveling alone, and one can only guess what thoughts and fears buffeted him. With the train carrying him farther away from home and everything familiar, speeding towards a strange place, his mind must have been buzzing with questions. *Will the doctors be able to fix my eyes? What will it be like working in Amana? Will I fit in? When will I see my family next?*

Michael and his parents had recently moved from Russia to South Dakota. At twenty years old, he was settling into his new home with his parents. They had just moved to their young colony in Bon Homme County when a dust storm blew through their community, severely damaging Michael's eyes.

Some thirty years earlier, the Amana Colonies, a Christian community of German Pietists, had established themselves in seven villages in Iowa. The Amana Colonies were founded in 1843–44 when this group, led by Christian Metz, fled Germany because of persecution and an economic depression. They first settled in Buffalo, New York. However, when they needed more farmland in 1855, they moved to Iowa, farming and living in community of goods along the Iowa River.

Amana members, sometimes called Inspirationists, were well established in America by the time the Hutterites arrived from Russia, and they kindly helped the Hutterites as they struggled to start new colonies. Along with supporting the Hutterites financially, Amana gave them supplies from their stores. On one occasion they provided the Hutterites with bolts of black-and-white polka-dot fabric, which was used for *Tiechlen* (head coverings) for the women. Thus, a Hutterite tradition was born, which in some colonies is still alive today. Prior to that, they used plain black fabric, which many Hutterites in recent years have been using again. It's quite possible that the use of sunbonnets for garden labor in previous generations was also something the Hutterites learned from the Amana Colonies, since this type of head covering is what Amana women traditionally wore.

It is no surprise, then, that when Michael Hofer's eyes were damaged, the Hutterites once again turned to Amana for assistance. Since Michael's Hutterite colony found no one in South Dakota who could help heal his eyes, the community opted to send him to the Amana Colonies, where they had their own doctors. This found Michael on a train, bound for Amana, where he would work in the community to pay for his eye treatment.

Under the excellent care of an Amana doctor, his eyes were soon restored to good health. However, he did not return home as expected. In 1880, obviously content with the Inspirationists' way of life, he chose to stay and made Amana his home, thus leaving one Christian community for another one.

Michael Hofer, a Hutterite who joined the Amana Colonies in Iowa.

\*   \*   \*

Michael Hofer lived in Main Amana, one of the seven villages in Iowa. Some years after joining the Inspirationists, he met Maria Stuck, a young woman from his own Amana village, while drawing water at a well. When I first learned about this, a song we usually sing at weddings came to mind. The song is based on the Bible story about Isaac's family servant, Eliezer, meeting Rebekah at the well and arranging for her to marry Isaac.

When Michael and Maria made their intentions of marriage known, they had to live in separate villages because of a customary yearlong separation that was required to test their commitment to marriage. Thus Maria went to Middle Amana and worked in the communal kitchen while Michael remained in Main Amana, working in the machine shop and woolen mill. I'm not sure if visits between engaged couples were normally allowed during this yearlong separation. However, Michael did visit Maria, sometimes trudging across a frozen pond during winter to do so. They were married October 4, 1888, and were assigned a home in Main Amana. They were blessed with two daughters, Susanna and Katharina.

Michael lived in Amana for the rest of his life, but stayed in contact with his Hutterite family, mainly through letters. At age sixty-five, in February 1924, he became very ill and was taken to an Iowa hospital where he had an appendectomy, complicated by pneumonia. He seemed to be doing fine, but then suddenly got worse and died that same evening. He was laid to rest in his home village, Main Amana. A simple memorial stone marks the final resting place of Michael Hofer. As was customary, the marker is identical to all the other markers in the Amana cemetery.

After her husband's death, Maria Hofer moved to Homestead, another Amana village, where her daughters lived with their families. She passed away in 1948. The daughters kept up contact with their Hutterite relatives until 1987, when Katharina Moershal died. Michael Hofer's niece Maria Hofer, who lived on my colony, corresponded with Katharina for many years. It's unfortunate, though, that there's no trace of the letters, for they would surely add some rich details to this story.

Through an online article, however, I got to know a great-granddaughter of Michael and Maria Hofer. Susan Sevig shared my excitement when I told her that I was a Hutterite. "I've always had a keen interest in my great-grandfather's people," she wrote. She kindly answered all my questions and provided me with pictures and other documents. Susan grew up in Amana but now lives in Arizona.

Three sons of Michael Hofer's niece Maria Hofer still live here at my colony. This fact fueled my interest in Amana and this fascinating story. It is still on my bucket list to visit Amana one day.

There are quite a few similarities between Amana and the Hutterites, including a German background and the history of fleeing to America because of persecution. For many years the Inspirationists also had "all things common," but they abandoned communal living because financial difficulties during the Great Depression in the 1930s. While Hutterites still live in Christian community and are largely farmers, Amana today is mainly a tourist attraction in Iowa, and is known for its restaurants and craft shops. In 1965, the colonies were listed as a national historic landmark.

It's interesting how things turned out: the Amana Colonies helped the Hutterites get started in America, but they ended up abandoning communal living. I sometimes wonder if the Hutterites could have helped the Colonies through their struggles. We aren't perfect, but we have figured out a few aspects of what works and what doesn't in living communally. Many experiments in Christian community have not lasted, and we are humbly grateful that our communities, with all their ongoing struggles, have remained strong and viable through all these centuries.

# 20

# A Hutterite Story of Slavery

*They went about in sheepskins and goatskins, destitute, perse-*
*cuted and mistreated—the world was not worthy of them.*
—Hebrews 11:37-38

I'VE BEEN BLOGGING since the spring of 2011. I began
after a local writer had read one of my articles in a newspaper
and sent me an email: "Linda, I really enjoyed your recent article! You should start your own blog. People would enjoy reading about your unique life." I had been thinking about that, but
the fact that I consider myself technologically challenged kept
me from even trying. Thus I was glad for the nudge and vote of
confidence. Before long I realized blogging is not that difficult
and could be a good platform for my writing, especially since I
could interact with my readers via comments and email.

Since I entered the blogosphere, I've received some remark-
able messages. None has been more fascinating than one from
a man in the United Kingdom. Reading it, I blinked a few
times before reading the note again. I wondered if this person
was dreaming.

Upon conducting an Internet search to learn more about the
Hutterer Park in Innsbruck, Austria, this person was led to my

blog. I had written a post on this park after visiting the area on a trip to Europe. He wrote:

> Hi Linda, Just read your "Living What Our Forefathers Died For" post. It's a deeply touching article, as I am a descendant of the Hutterites enslaved by Turks during the raids. We were eventually sold as slaves in Istanbul and sent to Cyprus. We were freed in the 1800s and still live in the same Turkish village in Cyprus. We are still in touch with our distant relatives in Süd Tirol [part of Italy] and some Hutterites around the world. I am keen to visit a Hutterite colony one day.

Naturally my curiosity was piqued. *Hutterite descendants in Cyprus?* I was aware of Hutterites being dragged away and sold into slavery but had never heard about what happened to them. *Do they still feel Hutterite or practice any remnant of Hutterite faith?* I wondered. *Did they ever try to return to their Hutterite community?* These questions compelled me to respond and find out more about this intriguing descendant of the Hutterites.

Over the course of a few emails, I learned that the man was born to Turkish Cypriot parents and was raised in the United Kingdom, where he was now living. "Since a very young age, I have always had a fascination with genealogy and trying to trace my ancestry," he wrote in an email. "I managed to trace my family tree back to the 1800s, to the same Turkish village my father is from, but couldn't go back any further. So I decided to take a DNA test to work out my origins. The results came, and it turns out I have the rarest European DNA (Haplogroup L2) and the DNA I carry only appears in one part of Europe: Süd Tirol."

A few years after my new friend had gotten this DNA test done, another man from Süd Tirol, an independent province

View of the farm in Cyprus where Hutterite descendants still live.

in northern Italy, took the same test. His results were posted onto a database, and because they matched, both men, one in the United Kingdom and the other in Süd Tirol, were alerted to this. They received an email from the DNA testing company to inform them they were twelfth cousins and shared the same forefather in the 1500s. At that point the man in the United Kingdom got in touch with this distant relative in Süd Tirol. Later, fascinated by this discovery, and wanting to learn more, he also visited him in Italy.

After more research, the two relatives learned that in the late 1500s their common ancestor lived on a farm in Leifers, Süd Tirol. One of their forefather's sons became a believer and converted to Anabaptism. Due to this, he was disowned by his family, left the farm, and went through severe persecution. The family who remained on the farm are the ancestors of the man in Süd Tirol. My friend in the United Kingdom descends from the disowned son who became an Anabaptist.

The trail then goes to Moravia, in the modern-day Czech Republic. This is where in the early 1600s, during the Turkish War, the Turks invaded and enslaved 240 Hutterites. This event is recorded in our history book, *The Chronicle of the Hutterian Brethren*. From Moravia they were taken to Hungary and then Istanbul, Turkey, where they were sold as slaves to a farm in Cyprus. The farm they settled on is the farm where the family continues to live today!

I've read a number of books on slavery, including the *The Emancipation of Robert Sadler*. I'm always deeply saddened by how people could be so cruel, demoralize other human beings, and think that they have the right to make them their slaves. However, I don't always pause and reflect that slavery was a part of my own history as well. It's this historic connection that touched me deeply when this man told me his story.

Nothing however, touched me as much as when we were discussing his last name and the fact that it never appears in our *Chronicle of the Hutterian Brethren*. "My surname is very unique. Because my ancestors were slaves, we were not allowed surnames; our surname was our father's first name," he explained. I could almost hear the sadness in his voice, even though I was reading this in an email. "My great-grandfather married a Jewish lady who was not a slave and who of course had a surname. Because of this my grandfather, although a Hutterite descendant, got this surname which has remained with me. So I have a Jewish surname. Now you can see why I cling to my Hutterite heritage so much. At long last I have an identity, which is why I started searching for my ancestry in the first place."

The sentence "We were not allowed surnames" made me want to weep. It was another level of cruelty to our ancestors we had never heard about. It's hard to fathom what that must have felt like. Not only were they slaves, but their very identity was trampled on as well. I am extremely grateful that this blog contact has made me study this chapter of our history in our *Chronicle of the Hutterian Brethren*. Here's an excerpt:

> Let us never forget those who were carried off into foreign parts, but continually remember them before God and daily bemoan their suffering. About 240 brothers, sisters and children were taken from us as prisoners. About 90 were eventually released, some as late as 1614. But there are about 150 of whom we heard no more. We have never found out whether they are still alive or where they may be scattered. What happened at that time was so dreadful, inhuman, and unchristian that it defies description. This is only a brief report, included here for the sake of our descendants. May God the Almighty grant them a better future.

"So, I am a descendant of the Hutterites who were freed from Turkish captivity," wrote my new friend. "As a result of my research and findings, I converted and became a believer, too. I now attend an Anabaptist Church in the UK; unfortunately, we have no Hutterite colonies here! My biggest motivation is to find all the lost Hutterites and give them the opportunity to return to Christ and to also have modern Hutterites know that regardless of all the hardships, we have survived." He is planning to write a book about his family's experiences, which he hopes will help him get in touch with other "lost Hutterites."

In a discussion regarding other Christian communities, I told him about the Bruderhof, which has a community in London, England. He has since made contact with former

Hutterites who live there and has visited them as well. He told me that these contacts have made him feel "very emotional and happy."

"There are no modern-day Hutterites from this same family line—they were all either murdered or enslaved by the Turks," my friend noted. "We have unfortunately lost our link, but I am intent on making the link again and ensuring the people from my father's village are made aware of their Hutterite origins. I am very keen to visit a colony and experience the life I call home!"

In his quest to find other "Turkish Hutterites," he has managed to find members of the Stahl family living in northeast Turkey. There are still many Stahls living in Hutterite colonies in Canada and the United States. As a result of this discovery he now plans to trace as many of the lost Turkish Hutterites as possible. In this work, he'll be following the footsteps and continuing the work of Salomon Böger, a Hutterite in Moravia who is mentioned briefly in *The Chronicle of the Hutterian Brethren*. Böger was known for his unusual and valiant efforts to redeem Hutterite women dragged away by the Turks during a very bloody raid in 1605. His wife and daughter were victims of these raids, which explains his passion to find and try to bring home these slaves. This mission lasted a few years. Ultimately he was able to reunite a few lost women with the community, but not his own family. In 1610 while traveling toward Hungary, he disappeared, and later it was reported he was murdered on the road.

Having recently visited Moravia, today known as the Czech Republic, I found my interest piqued by this story. It is a part of Hutterite history that never made it into our history books because tragically, people sometimes just disappeared and were never heard of again—until now, thanks to my UK friend. In reading our history, I've often wondered what happened to the people who, by choice or by force, were separated from their Hutterite communities. For example, what happened to the people who chose to stay in Russia when the Hutterites immigrated to America? The Cyprus connection makes me wonder what more we'll learn, given the information age in which we live.

# 21

# *Following the Footsteps of Our Forebears*

*Let them look to the past, but let them also look to the future;*
*let them look to the land of their ancestors,*
*but let them look also to the land of their children.*
—Wilfrid Laurier, Canada's seventh prime minister, 1896–1911

**I READ THE EMAIL TWICE** to make sure I understood this right. Yes, this really is a scholarship opportunity in Germany. Carpe diem! I could either let this chance slip away or I could "seize the day." I decided on the latter, and I soon realized that sometimes when you walk through an open door, God has more blessings in store!

Thus a colleague and I accepted a scholarship for a teaching methods course, offered by the Lower Saxony Ministry of Education. We'd be studying in Hannover, Germany, for ten days, with hotel, food, and local transportation provided.

The scholarship itself was worth celebrating. But when I found out later that we could also do a Hutterite history tour through several European countries prior to our course, my excitement doubled. Strong supporters of education, our community leaders gave their blessing for the trip. August found five of us—my sister and three friends—flying to Zurich, Switzerland, the birthplace of the Anabaptist movement in the 1500s. This radical wing of the Reformation included groups that believed in living "all things common," as practiced in biblical times and described in Acts 2:42-47.

Hearing and reading the stories from our history since childhood had instilled in me a longing to visit the land of our forebears. However, I had never imagined that the opportunity would actually come without any plans on my part.

The tour took us to Switzerland, Austria, Italy, Slovakia, the Czech Republic, and then finally Germany for our course. "We're taking an intensive church history course," someone in our group remarked as we traveled, and the rest of us wholeheartedly agreed. Packed into eleven days were visits to the places connected to the Reformation, some of which evoked strong emotions. Anabaptist beginnings and specifically early Hutterite settlements included places where severe persecution, lengthy imprisonments, and brutal deaths occurred. These challenges ultimately led to all Hutterites fleeing from one European country to another until they settled in Russia in 1762. A hundred years later, Hutterites were once again forced to leave their home, this time to America. Many would eventually settle in Canada.

In Europe, we met two different committees who work diligently to ensure that the Anabaptist story is not forgotten. With government grants, one committee in Vienna, Austria, has set up two museums of Anabaptist and Hutterite history in Lower Austria, one at the ruins of the Falkenstein Castle, and the other in the Sulz Weinviertel. Another committee is hoping to

Schloss Taufers in Süd Tirol, Italy, a castle where early Hutterites were imprisoned.

open the Hutterer Park in Innsbruck, Austria, to commemorate Anabaptists who died for their faith. The park is right along the Inn River, where many believers were drowned. I was deeply touched when visiting these places, as our hosts read us the stories from our *Chronicle of the Hutterian Brethren*.

One of the places we saw was the ruins of Schloss Rattenberg, where seventy-one Anabaptists were beheaded in one day. It's a steep climb, part crude steps and part narrow trail, and we had to stop to catch our breaths every so often. There was ample time to ponder the plight of our forebears and what it cost them to walk this trail. Once we were at the top and saw the remains of this castle up close, a heaviness that's hard to describe settled over me. The horror of the things that happened here suddenly became more real. Our tour guide gave us time to reflect what it cost the martyrs to stand up for biblical truths.

In Süd Tirol, Italy, we toured Schloss Taufers, where Hans Kräl suffered horribly, imprisoned in a dungeon. Between 1578 and 1583, Kräl was the head of the Hutterian brotherhood in Moravia, today the Czech Republic. The part of the castle where the dungeon is located is deemed unsafe, and out of bounds for visitors. However, our tour guide told us, "Since we have Hutterites in our group, I will let you see it." We couldn't go down into the dungeon but stood at the opening long enough to take some pictures and ponder this heartrending story from our *Chronicle of the Hutterian Brethren*:

> His greatest sorrow was that no messages got through to him from the church. At that time Hans Mändl, a servant of the Lord's Word, was in the mountains of Tirol. He had a great longing for news from Hans Kräl and got word to him in the dungeon, asking him to send some sign that he was still faithful to God and his church. If he had nothing else, he should send a little bundle of straw. Hans Kräl would gladly have done so, but he did not even have so much as a bundle of straw in the dungeon. That is how poor he was. Then he remembered the collar of his rotted shirt, which he had hung on the wall, and glad that he had it, he took it down and sent it to the brothers as a sign that he was at peace with God and the church. When they received the collar and saw how destitute he was, it went to their hearts and they wept out of pity for him. They sent a message back to him in the dungeon that they would be more than happy to send him a shirt or anything else, if only they knew how. But he did not want them to try, because if it were discovered he would be tortured again and those who brought it would have to suffer. So he let them know that they should not send him anything. He must clothe himself with the garment of patience.

One of the buildings at a former Hutterite colony, Sabatisch, Czech Republic.

On July 29, 1546, the Hutterites bought an undeveloped mill at Sabatisch, in today's Czech Republic. They converted it into dwellings and lived there under the protection of Franz Niáry at Branc. I was excited to visit this former Hutterite community, especially since Maendels once lived there. The building structures still seemed sturdy, but they looked rundown and were not inhabited. The doors were locked and some windows boarded up, so we couldn't go inside. But Velkè Lèware, another former community in Slovakia, is totally restored, and people are living in the homes. Here too we were not able to go inside, but we walked around and admired the buildings from the outside. In both places I found it hard to imagine Hutterites living there. I wondered what it would be like to live there today. Would there be Hutterites in Europe today if our forebears had not been driven from these places?

As I reflect on those three memorable weeks, I'm thankful that my community granted me this amazing opportunity to enhance not only my German but also my knowledge of church history. I came away with a deep gratitude for the freedom of religion we enjoy today, a renewed appreciation for the legacy our ancestors left us, and some lingering questions. Are we diligent enough in keeping this torch of faith aflame? While our forebears suffered severe persecution, we live comfortably. We relish a high standard of living, taking so much for granted, and, too often, exhibit petty grievances.

I'm also grateful for many new friends in Europe. We're now connected through our history, and we are able to enjoy what our forebears died for—freedom to serve God peacefully and share the story of salvation with others. One of our new friends from Austria shared these sentiments: "These visits are a blessing. Not only do they allow us to establish beautiful friendships, but also, little by little, heal the deep wounds of the Anabaptist persecutions of our country's history."

# 22

# *Love without End*

*Beautiful is the man who leaves a legacy that of shared love and life. It is he who transfers meaning, assigns significance and conveys in his loving touch, the fine art and gentle shaping of a life. This man shall be called, Father.*

—Stella Payton, author and speaker

ANOTHER FATHER'S DAY WITHOUT DAD. It has been more than ten years since he died. On days like this, when I miss him the most, I like to tell stories—an activity that he helped cultivate.

I have so many wonderful memories of my dad, and I know I was blessed to have him near for many years, especially when I consider others who were young children when they lost their fathers. I recently talked with a young mother who had lost her husband. She was telling me how hard it is for her young children when they make Father's Day cards in school. "They can't decide who to give the card to," she said. "When looking for verses to write inside the card, they all are clearly written for dads, and not so much for someone who is [now] the father figure in their lives."

"Have them write from their hearts, and then they'll have words that convey exactly how they feel," I suggested.

"That's a good idea," she responded. "They always end up giving one card to me, since I'm both Mom and Dad, and one to their grandpa, who plays an important role in their life."

While planting petunias on Dad's grave in spring, I remembered how he always encouraged us to have some kind of hobby, whether crafts or collections. Once we had found a hobby, he'd always find ways to nurture the interest. During my teenage years, he must have overheard me say that I'd love to have Aunt Susie, an expert in many crafts, teach me to crochet an afghan but that I didn't have any wool. So one day he came home from Winnipeg with a bag of wool for me. I'm still amazed today how well the colors complemented each other. One was my favorite color, grass green, and the other two were bright yellow and dark brown.

Aunt Susie now had a student, to whom she patiently passed on the skill of crocheting. For my afghan, I chose a common and fairly easy zigzag pattern, which took me many weeks to complete. I admit that sometimes, for days on end, I'd stay away from my new hobby. But Dad kept asking how far along the afghan was and reminding me, "*Wer longsum foet, kummt ach on Oet*" (Going slowly gets the job done too). Going slowly did indeed get the job done, and once that day arrived, Dad was as proud of it as I was.

Looking back today, I understand why he was so proud. I was learning a useful craft and spending quality time at my grandparents' house, where Aunt Susie also lived and taught me the art of crochet. I kept the afghan for many years, and when I no longer used it, Mom was right there to unravel all my hard work. Like a mama on a mission, she gave the wool a new purpose: to keep toes warm, as knitted slippers.

\* \* \*

On a Hutterite colony it's very common for members to volunteer at different tasks in addition to their daily duties. I've been tending the flowers at the community cemetery. I love the tranquility there, especially in the evening when the sun sinks low in the western sky. It creates lace-like shadows on the soft, cool grass.

From time to time, children come to help with mowing the lawn or weeding. One day two schoolboys worked with me. One of them proved to be a good little worker. But despite all my reprimands, the other one was clearly not in a working mood. The ripe raspberries that kept calling him from across the road didn't help either.

As we worked, the boys asked many questions about the people resting in the cemetery. Children always enjoy listening to these stories, especially if the person is a relative. "These markers are stones with stories," I told them. "This stone says Edward and Marvin Maendel. They're my little brothers who died in a house fire many years ago." The boys were silent. The past touched the present for a moment.

One year, my mom, aunt Margaret, and I were planting flowers on the graves when the German teacher stopped by. "I think you could use some help here. I'll go round up some boys for you," he offered.

"That should go well," I chuckled as I watched him leave. "I wonder if he knows what he's up against. He'll have to break up the Hutterite Grey Cup Game of summer." Watching them, you'd think there's almost as much at stake as in the Canadian Football League's Grey Cup game.

Nevertheless, in a few minutes, I was pleasantly surprised when a parade of bikes headed our way. "How did you pull this off?" I asked.

"Wasn't too difficult," their teacher said. "I just told them you needed help and that with so many working together, not much precious game time would be lost." Soon the place was bustling like a beehive. Some were planting and watering, while others were digging around the trees and adding rich soil from the cow pasture. Before long, the boys could return to the battle for bragging rights, with their impromptu, longer-than-usual half-time intermission behind them.

"Community action," I mused when we were all done. It's another reminder of how invaluable multiple generations are to our communal life. In working together, tenets of our faith, values, work ethic, culture, and heritage are passed on to our children. Bridging past with present, gravestones evoke memories of those who walked before us and who call us to continue their legacy: "impress them on your children. Talk about them when you sit at home and when you walk along the road, when you lie down and when you get up" (Deuteronomy 6:7).

Dad, who lived by the maxim "*Arbeit macht das Leben süß*" (Work makes life sweet), must have been smiling. Working together, three generations had transformed our cemetery, adding lovely splashes of color to the neatly trimmed carpet of grass.

# FAQS ABOUT THE HUTTERITES

# The Author Answers

*Author Linda Maendel answers some frequently asked questions about Hutterite life, faith, and culture.*

**1. Do you really share everything—including things like clothes, pots and pans, furniture?**

No. For the most part, what is in Hutterite homes is considered the personal property of the family or individuals. Hutterite families live in their own modern homes provided by the colony. It's common for people to share with others from their personal possessions, however, when the need arises. All Hutterites, however, share things like the laundry facilities, communal kitchen, and vehicles with everybody else in the community.

**2. Who makes decisions about how money is used on a Hutterite colony?**

The brotherhood, or all baptized men, make decisions concerning the purchase or construction of large items, such as farm machinery, vehicles, or building homes and barns. But for smaller, everyday purchases for communal and personal needs—such as toiletry items, snacks, and cleaning supplies—the community relies on the *Hausholter* (financial manager) and his wife. It's also the *Hausholter* who provides us with money when we go on any kind of trips, such as appointments, visiting, or work-related conferences or meetings. The *Hausholter*, once elected, holds that position until he feels he's unable to do so anymore, say, for health reasons.

### 3. Do Hutterites pay taxes?

Yes, Hutterites pay taxes just like everybody else. Colonies pay taxes on net income divided among all colony workers over the age of eighteen. Taxes are determined by dividing total colony income by the number of residents, then adding deductions. They pay income tax, sales tax, school tax, and health, education, and property taxes.

Dating back as far 1590, Hutterites agreed to pay taxes provided that the money was not used for war purposes. At that time, when Hutterites refused to pay taxes that went to the military, authorities confiscated communal property such as livestock. After repeated requests to consider paying taxes, Hutterian elders unanimously agreed "that it was only fair, as we benefitted from the country, that we should also contribute something." In a letter to Lord Friedrich von Zerotin at Seelwitz they wrote, "We would be willing to pay an annual sum . . . as long as we can be assured that the money will be used profitably for the country and for people in need."

### 4. Do individual Hutterites have their own spending money and bank accounts?

As suggested above, we do have some spending money. This is given to us by the *Hausholter* as we need it, and especially when we leave the colony for an appointment or to go shopping. Because the community supplies our needs, however, we believe that a personal bank account would contradict the New Testament teachings (particularly Acts 2:40-47) upon which Hutterian communal life is based.

### 5. Do outsiders ever join Hutterite colonies? If so, what do they have to do to prepare to join?

It happens, but not very often. Some people have joined the Hutterites and are very content with their decision to live in Christian community. New people interested in joining are generally invited to come and try communal life to see if that is what they really desire. For most people, it would be a very different life from what they're accustomed to and would likely involve a difficult adjustment to the religious practices and the unique culture—including the use of a dialect in daily life and the German church services.

### 6. What is a church service like on a Hutterite colony?

Most of our services are conducted in German, although English is occasionally used in some communities. Evening vespers services (*Gebet*) are a half hour, while the Sunday morning service (*Lehr*) is an hour or longer. Each service begins with a German hymn. Most sermons are used as they were written by our forebears; they are in Old High German and include Scripture readings with detailed commentary. Often ministers will add their own thoughts as well. A prayer is always part of the service, which is how the evening service concludes. The Sunday morning service ends with congregational singing, followed by a benediction.

### 7. Is it accurate to say that Hutterite life is "plain"?

That would depend on what is meant by "plain." If it means dressing modestly—women wearing long dresses and little to no jewelry or makeup, and men usually attired in dark trousers and button-down shirts—then I would agree we're plain. If it means living without modern conveniences or technology, I would have to disagree. We drive modern vehicles; farm with the best machinery; construct state-of-the-art shops and barns and spacious modern homes, schools, and communal kitchens; and use the latest cooking and baking appliances.

Some would deem our church building plain; the walls are left bare and we don't have stained glass windows. For us, it's a place of worship and is kept relatively simple, though many colony churches now have carpet and most have upholstered pews. Traditionally, our forebears insisted on church buildings that were as simple as any other building on the *Hof*, the community. Their tenet was that the church that is pleasing to God is not a building; rather, it is the people who compose the actual church. However, the newer churches being built today are considerably larger and grander, with high, even slightly vaulted ceilings and distinctive windows.

### 8. What are some challenges Hutterites face with regard to technology?

While Hutterites enjoy the benefits of technology daily, there's no doubt that it will be one of our biggest challenges. The future of the Hutterite people will depend on our ability to use technology, in harmony with our vision as a Christian community. To face these challenges, it's imperative that parents and teachers are in sync with this vision and are united in our commitment to raise children who will become future pillars of their church community. Children and young people need to be surrounded by positive role models who practice using technology wisely.

Two issues we are wrestling with are the type of movies our children watch and the amount of time they spend with electronic games. There's concern about the negative influences they can have on our children. Are Hutterite parents, teachers, and other caregivers even aware of the influences? What happened to board games and jigsaw puzzles? I have many happy memories of sitting around the table with games like Sorry and Probe. Activities like these encourage healthy interaction with others and stimulate intellectual development; by contrast, electronic devices encourage people to block out everybody by staring at a screen for hours on end.

Recently a *Dariusleut* minister was asked about his views on the impact technology will have on Hutterites. His response left no doubt about how big of a challenge this is: "We've survived hundreds of years of severe persecution, but I don't think we'll survive this."

### 9. Some people say that Hutterites are buying all the farmland because they can outbid almost anyone else. Is that true?

Hutterites are largely farmers. To be sustainable and to remain abreast of inflation, Hutterites buy farmland. We will not pay more than the land is worth—to do so would guarantee our extinction. Farmers who live near a Hutterite colony are guaranteed fair-market value for their land when they decide to sell to Hutterites when they retire or move on to other ventures.

Some argue that permitting Hutterite colonies to expand will seriously threaten the family farm, claiming that the latter (even those which are in excess of thousands of acres in size) can't compete with the colonies. Actually, Hutterites are not in serious competition with anybody who wishes to purchase land. The main competition comes from farmers with a surplus of investment funds. Furthermore, the accusation begs the question whether Hutterites are more of a threat to smaller communities than local residents.

**10. Some claim Hutterites don't purchase implements and farm equipment locally or patronize local businesses. Is this true?**

When Hutterites purchase a piece of farm machinery, we acquire not only that implement or equipment but the service that comes with it. Today's farm machinery is not your grandpa's machinery. It is fully computerized, requiring highly trained personnel to troubleshoot and repair. Therefore, purchasing out of the local area would be counterproductive. As for patronizing local businesses, why would Hutterites drive out of the area to buy items, if they don't need to? Time and travel cost money! Also, consider that Hutterites stay on the farm year round: traveling to exotic destinations for weeks and months of vacation is not in our repertoire of behaviors. Consequently, most of our hard-earned money is spent locally.

In most cases, colonies spend far more in local communities than the farmers they may replace. The typical Hutterite colony supports lumber yards, fertilizer and chemical dealers, grocery stores, meat shops, drugstores, automotive shops, banks, veterinary clinics, farm equipment, vehicles, and grain and livestock dealers. Proprietors of such business attest to the fact that Hutterites are very important to the economy of smaller communities.

## 11. How frequently do you travel outside of your community?

Opportunities to travel outside of our community are legion: medical and dental appointments, conferences, seminars, visiting, shopping, blood donor clinics, singing in hospitals and seniors' residences, vegetable/herb/fruit picking, and school field trips. Hutterites are travelers! Family ties are strong, so visits to relatives in other, often remote colonies are a regular part of weekends and holy days such as Christmas, Easter, Ascension Day, and Pentecost.

Because Hutterites help each other, there are frequent opportunities to spend extended periods of time in another colony to help with the care of a sick relative, harvesting, building, or other work. There is also work-related travel, including making deliveries of livestock, grain, and manufactured goods and commodities. Attendance at international trade shows pertaining to business is becoming increasingly common.

The same holds true for young people. They might drive to another colony for the evening after attending a blood donor clinic; enjoy an outdoor swimming spot at another colony and then join them for a wiener roast supper, game of baseball, and a bonfire sing-along; meet at an urban arena for a hockey game; or attend a concert or drama. Another increasingly common practice is a summer bus tour of colony flower gardens, concluding with a barbecue at a colony or a local park. Clearly, such an outing is just an excuse for a ladies' afternoon out to enjoy a lovely summer day outdoors in each other's company!

# Author's Note

**TO MY READERS:** thank you for picking up this book and for your interest in my Hutterite life. I hope you found this collection of stories, newspaper articles, and blog posts interesting and inspiring and that you came away at least a little wiser, as the title promises. I also hope they gave you a glimpse of my Hutterite life—a life that, thus far, has rarely been written about by Hutterites themselves, at least in a published work. I love to write and am grateful to Herald Press for this opportunity to share my stories.

Working on this book has been an enriching and enjoyable experience. Thanks to my talented and patient editor, Valerie Weaver-Zercher, I learned so much about the writing and publishing process! With her superb guidance and advice the revising, rewriting, and in some cases, rethinking my work was pure pleasure, for I knew it meant I'd have a more entertaining and engaging read in the end.

If you find yourself named within these pages, I'm grateful to have you in my circle of family and friends; thank you for helping me share these stories. If you are Hutterite and can relate to some of the narratives, know that as I wrote, I was thinking not only of the people mentioned in my book but often of Hutterites in general, since we do share many of the same experiences.

My heartfelt thanks to my friends Dora Maendel and Paul Wipf, whom I could always count on for encouragement, sage advice, and availability to share ideas with, while I worked on this project.

For my four sweet front-cover girls—Daria, Jodi, Saphira, and Nicole—*Danke Schön* for agreeing to do this. You add life and color to my book!

I'm extremely grateful that I was born to dedicated Hutterite parents, giving me the opportunity to be a part of this Christian communal way of life I treasure. I appreciate that I can serve my community in our school and in any other way I'm able. I'm thankful for the gift of story, for it enriches my life—both in the reading and in the writing. I'm delighted that I can feel free to be creative with written language and thus share our unique way of life with others.

*—Linda Maendel*

# The Author

**LINDA MAENDEL** is a Hutterite author, blogger, and educator. She lives in the Elm River Colony outside of Winnipeg, Manitoba. Her writing has appeared in the *Winnipeg Free Press*, *Our Canada*, the *Portage Daily Graphic*, the *Manitoba Cooperator*, and *Deutsche Rundschau*. She has also written a German children's book about Hutterite life and translated Bible stories into Hutterisch, the language of the Hutterites. Maendel has lived her entire life in the same Hutterite community, where she teaches German and English to children in kindergarten through grade eight. She blogs at www.hutt-writevoice.blogspot.com.